Secrets Under the Parking Lot

Secrets Under the Parking Lot

Revised Edition

The True Story of Upper Arlington, Ohio, and the
History of Perry Township in the Nineteenth Century

DIANE KELLY RUNYON AND KIM SHOEMAKER STARR

Copyright © 2019 Diane Kelly Runyon and Kim Shoemaker Starr

All rights reserved. This book or any portion thereof may not be reproduced or used in any manner whatsoever without the express written permission of the publisher.

Printed in the United States of America

First Printing, 2016

ISBN: 1698955452
ISBN 13: 9781698955452
Library of Congress Control Number: 2019917417
CreateSpace Independent Publishing Platform
North Charleston, South Carolina

Typeset by Amnet Systems

This book is dedicated to Pleasant Litchford and all the people he influenced in his life.

"We are chosen, to breathe life into all who have gone before."

Contents

Preface · xi
Acknowledgments · xiii
Introduction · xv

One   What Made Up Perry Township? · · · · · · · · · · · 1
What Would It Be Like to Live in Rural
Franklin County, Ohio, in the Nineteenth Century? · 4
Travel in Early Ohio · 5
Everyday Life · 14
Revolutionary War Patriots and Pioneers of
Perry Township, Franklin County, Ohio · · · · · · · 28
Amaziah Hutchinson · · · · · · · · · · · · · · · · · · · 28
Elijah Backus · 30
The Delashmutt, McCoy, and Richards Families · · 33
The Walcott, Legg, and Slyh Families · · · · · · · · · 37
John and Ann Simpson Davis · · · · · · · · · · · · · 42
Rudolph Phenegar · 45
William Neil · 47

Two   A United, Not Divided, Community. Black
History in Perry Township. · · · · · · · · · · · · · · · 49

	The Pleasant Litchford Story Born a Slave, Died a Millionaire · · · · · · · · · · · · · · · · · · 49
	Pleasant Litchford's Family · · · · · · · · · · · · · · · · 57
	Perry Township's Colored School · · · · · · · · · · · · 64
	James Poindexter · 67
	Negro Woman Becomes Heiress · · · · · · · · · · · · 72
	The Story of Catherine Litchford Walker · · · · · · · 72
	Inherits an Estate · 73
	Negro Woman to Get Fortune · · · · · · · · · · · · · 76
	She is in Possession · · · · · · · · · · · · · · · · · · · 78
	C. Walker Resorts to Strategy · · · · · · · · · · · · · · 80
	William H. Litchferd · · · · · · · · · · · · · · · · · · · 83
	Litchford Hotel · 83
	William Hannibal Thomas · · · · · · · · · · · · · · · 86
	Lucy Depp Settlement · · · · · · · · · · · · · · · · · 88
	Second Baptist Church · · · · · · · · · · · · · · · · · 90
Three	The Unknown Legacy of Upper Arlington
	Twentieth Century Reality of Perry Township · · · · 95
	Ben and King Thompson Social Engineering · · · · 95
	Sundown Town · 101
	Litchford Cemetery Relocated · · · · · · · · · · · · · 103
	2017 Upper Arlington Board of Education · · · · · · 112
	Pleasant Litchford's Landholdings · · · · · · · · · · · 113
	Sources and Citations · · · · · · · · · · · · · · · · · · 115
	Bibliography · 123
	Index · 129
	Disclaimer for historical materials · · · · · · · · · · · 137
	About the Authors · 139

Preface

Often, we are asked how this journey had all started. Why did we end up writing a book on this subject? My close friend, Kim Starr is a headstone restoration specialist and she lived across the street from the Litchford Cemetery when she was young. Since we are both cemetery lovers, we were curious what happened to this burial site, because it no longer was there. So, Kim asked me to see if I could find a name of a black family that lived there. That question at the MCL cafeteria in Upper Arlington was the beginning of everything.

Being Perry Township, it was not hard to find black families on the 1860-1870 census, since it was predominately white. The name that reoccurred was Litchford. Then it took a year of on-site research to find the information that we have presented. We are very grateful to the people in the acknowledgments that also worked with us side by side to find these documents. As of this reprinting this book research is still in progress and an archeological survey and assessment of the properties will be continuing for the next few years.

This book has been a period of enlightenment and understanding of what obstacles and prejudices against certain individuals that were Black and Jewish in this community during the 20th century. Education does not provide an enough accurate instruction on these subjects. We have found that not only the white population was surprised at the presence of the Green Book, but so are young black students. If we do not teach our past, we repeat those mistakes in the future.

Respectfully,
    Diane Kelly Runyon
    Author/Genealogist

Acknowledgments

There are so many people to thank who have been a big part of this research, first and foremost, the History and Genealogy Department of the Columbus Metropolitan Library and the African American Genealogy Group. The researchers there have been strong supporters of this book and the contents in it. The wonderful librarians we want to thank are, Russ Pollit, Julia Callahan, Nick Taggart, Scott Caputo, Arron O'Donovan, and Chuck Cody. We also want to thank the Ohio Historical Society, Sandra Jamison, Reita Smith, Nettie Ferguson, Kathy Nelson and the Second Baptist Church and all the wonderful people in their congregation.

The Underground Railroad Museum, Neil Bryant, great grandson of Pleasant Litchford, Mary Rogers from Union Cemetery, Billy Martin from Rutherford Funeral Home, Scott Bowman, Franklin Co. Recorders Office and our families and friends, who are too numerous to mention.

We are grateful and blessed to have this opportunity to write this book so that the story of Perry Township in the nineteenth century will be forever documented as well as the people who lived there and made this wilderness their home.

DEATH CERTIFICATE.

(ATTENDING PHYSICIAN.)

Name Pleasant Stockford
Age 89 years Nativity Lynchburgh Va.
Sex Male Color Black Married or Single Married
Place of death Madison Cause of death Old Age
Date of death April 6th 1879
Duration of last illness ——— Post-mortem No
made ———

Jas. R. Lewis M. D.
Residence,

(UNDERTAKER'S.)

Died at No. West   Street
Buried at Columbus Ohio   Cemetery
Date of burial Apr 7 1879
C. V. L. Undertaker.
Issued to Jas R Lewis M. D.

Introduction

This book is a movement across time to weave together a story of the lives that unfolded in Perry Township, Franklin County, Ohio, during the nineteenth century. The township was a unified group of pioneers from all walks of life, ethnic cultures, and races. These settlers worked together to create homes and farms from complete wilderness. People of color were among them, as part of the culture and the early history of what is now twenty-first entury Upper Arlington, Ohio. The most compelling story is about Pleasant Litchford and his family, free people of color who came to Perry Township from Virginia in 1830. Pleasant Litchford died fifty years later, a millionaire. His story has been silenced to hide the fact that the very people who were denied property ownership after 1915 had been there since the early days of statehood. This story reveals the underlying silent conversation of racism and the rule of exclusionary property ownership, which was to be in effect until 1990. In 1970, the Ohio Supreme Court ruled against the Northwest Arlington Homeowners Association, in a lawsuit over the association's policy of excluding certain populations from property ownership.

Around the period of 1913–15, unfortunate policies changed when socially engineered philosophies by King and Ben Thompson changed the racial conversation. Much of this book is based on never before researched documentation to provide an accurate representation of a rural area of Franklin County and the people who lived there. This book stems from a belief that we should honor those who have gone before us, to honor our military soldiers and never forget the people who started their lives in the wilderness of Ohio.

Let it be understood that this book's purpose is not to cast a negative light upon the city of Upper Arlington, Ohio. The main focus is to tell an intriguing story about a former slave and his family's walk through life during the nineteenth century in what would become Upper Arlington. Covenants and Sundown Towns, had the purpose of keeping certain minorities out of white neighborhoods, existed throughout the country. Upper Arlington was not alone in the practice of excluding people of color from property ownership. Pleasant Litchford's property and his family's burial place are important topics of contemporary times; I am sure their legacy will be secured.

(1) Patent to Cyrus Riley 22 Sept 1800

JOHN ADAMS, President of the United States of America,

To all to whom these presents shall come, Greeting:

Know ye, That in pursuance of the act of Congress passed on the first day of June 1796, entitled "An Act regulating the grants of Land appropriated for Military services, and of the several acts supplementary thereto passed on the second day of March 1799, and on the eleventh day of February and first of March 1800, there is granted unto Cyrus Riley _____ a certain tract of land estimated to contain Two thousand nine hundred seventy nine and sixty four hundredth acres being the fourth Quarter of the five township in The Nineteenth Range of the tract appointed for satisfying Warrants for Military service; which lying in the State is as respondant for four thousand acres _____ ", surveyed and located in pursuance of the acts above recited: TO HAVE and to HOLD the said described tract of land, with the appurtenances thereof unto the said Cyrus Riley, _____ " _____ and to __ his heirs and assigns forever, subject to the conditions, restrictions and provisions contained in the said recited acts.

In Witness whereof, the said John Adams, President of the United States of America, hath caused the Seal of the said United States to be hereunto affixed, and signed the same with his hand, at the City of Philadelphia the twentieth ~ day of Sept ~ in the year of our Lord 1800 ; and of the Independence of the United States of America the twenty fifth

John Adams

By the President,
Timothy Pickering

Secretary of State.

One

What Made Up Perry Township?

Perry Township is the township where Upper Arlington, Ohio, is located. In the beginning, the township was bound on the west by the Scioto River in what was called Range Nineteen. Range Nineteen was composed of two fractional original townships. Perry Township was a long township, ten miles from north to south, one mile wide at its narrowest point, and three miles wide at its widest point. The north end of Perry Township included Dublin and Worthington, and to the south were Grandview and Marble Cliff. The reason for the various widths is that the township bordered the Scioto River, which rambles throughout the state. It originally was surveyed as part of Liberty Township and then became part of Washington Township. In later years it was attached to Norwich Township. If you are researching records prior to 1820, then you should consider including these other townships because township boundaries were fluid during the early years of the county. After 1820, Perry Township was given its name, after Commodore Perry, and it remains Perry Township today.

The 1842 plat map shows more than forty landholders. You can see some of the original roads on the plat map. Tremont Road was also known as Worthington and Georgesville Road. A township road called Litchford Road was changed to Glouster Road and then to Ridgeview Road in September 1951. Dodridge Road was called the Jacob Slyh Road.

The 1872 plat map of Perry Township shows a list of thirty property owners in what is called the Backus tract. The Backus tract is located south of Fishinger Road.

The top five landowners on this list were as follows:

Henry Miller—800 acres
David Lakin—301 acres
J. Slyh – 283.5 acres
Pleasant Litchford – 271 acres
Hiram Richards – 214 acres

Perry Township was made up of a diverse collection of families from different ethnic backgrounds, beliefs, and races. They were Scots-Irish, English, French, and German, Italian and many were recently freed slaves looking for a new life on free soil. In analyzing the lives of the residents, one common thread came to light. A large majority of them had the same basic values, devotion to family, religion, and antislavery beliefs. They worked together to help each other survive a challenging environment.

Staying connected to home back East was sometimes hard to do. In 1805, the mail was carried from Franklinton to Chillicothe and back by a boy of thirteen years named A. McElvain. He was required to swim Darby and Deer Creeks while carrying mail bags on his back. Mail would come to Columbus once a month and the person who received the letter had to pay twenty-five cents. Mail was not prepaid. There was no post office in Perry Township. If a person wanted to pick up any mail, he or she had to go to Worthington or Dublin. It was not until 1878, when the Toledo and Columbus Railroad was completed, that a mail stop nearby was established. It was called the Olentangy Post Office.

When settlers came to Perry Township, it was a virtual wilderness. They had to fell trees to build homes but also to clear land so they could grow crops to provide a subsistence living. Then, once they provided for their families, it was necessary to prepare more land to provide an income. It was not an easy life.

The Underground Railroad was active in Perry Township. The Litchford family was part of the Depp family through marriage. The Depps had one of the most active Underground Railroad stops in central Ohio. The Litchfords possessed a strong antislavery conviction and their participation in the process of transferring slaves to the Scioto River was known to their neighbors. They might not have housed slaves, but they knew about their activities and did not hinder the operation. Pleasant Litchford took those skills, and with smart strategies, community activism, and a keen business sense, over the course of fifty years, the slave born in Virginia in 1789 died a millionaire, in 1879.

The irony is that the land that he owned in Ohio for fifty years as a black man was later restricted by white elitists, who placed in their deeds a covenant that kept blacks from living there. They were already there, eighty years before Thompson's socially engineered community existed. Research has uncovered documents that had never before been brought to light, and some people would have preferred to keep them in the dark.

Diane Kelly Runyon and Kim Shoemaker Starr

What Would It Be Like to Live in Rural Franklin County, Ohio, in the Nineteenth Century?

Ohio, during that time, where these pioneers settled, was pure wilderness. For white settlers, Native Americans were their biggest challenge in establishing a settlement, but sheer survival in relocating to this land was daunting. Pioneers could travel the waterways, and the Monongahela and Ohio Rivers were their first routes of passage. All travel for transportation and goods to central Ohio was done via the Scioto, Little Miami, and Muskingum Rivers. It was very important to protect these waterways.

If you were a free person of color, your means of travel was any way you could find, no matter the danger. People of color knew that many opportunities were available in Ohio. Black families would travel from Virginia on the National Road or other, smaller roadways. Travel challenges did not deter these families from starting a new life far from Virginia slaveholders. Once they were freed, they had one year to leave the state.

Settlers looked for areas in close proximity to water since water was the key to a successful settlement. Ohio provided an abundance of fertile soil, which helped to make farming a prosperous occupation. The state was carpeted by dense forest except for the swamplands in the northwest. The forest teemed with wildlife, black bear, moose, elk, fox, muskrat, and many varieties of birds. Wonderful yellow salmon was plentiful in the Scioto River. By the turn of the twentieth century, the state was stripped of all forest, except for southeastern Ohio, but even there the forest was thinning out. Wood was used for mostly everything in daily living, including housing, warmth, cooking, and tools, and this renewable resource quickly disappeared, within just one hundred years. Reforestation has been slow. This meant that the region's animal life would also relocate to the West.

Travel in Early Ohio

Transportation was crude and often difficult. If you traveled prior to 1825, you traveled along the Ohio River or other rivers such as the Little Miami or Scioto to get to the interior of Ohio. They were narrow and winding, overgrown with brush and fallen trees. The topography was mountainous and was reduced to hills by the time you entered western Pennsylvania and southern Ohio.

What were the Indian trails that crisscrossed the Franklin County area? There were two major Indian trails that were traveled extensively by the tribes of the area. The Walhonding Trail departed from the Olentangy River and ran across north-west Franklin County, following the Salt Lick. This trail was a connection for the Delaware Indians living by the Scioto River and the Muskingum located in eastern Ohio. This area had settlements of Wyandots, Delaware, and Shawnee, and other smaller Indian tribes.

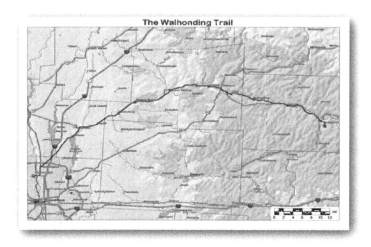

The other significant Indian trail that traversed Franklin County running north and south was the Scioto Trail, which was also called the Warrior's Path. This trail was considered the "Great Highway of the Shawnee." The Shawnee Indians, under the leadership of Tecumseh, Blue Jacket, and the Prophet, embraced this trail as a means to access fertile hunting grounds from Kentucky to Sandusky. This trail traveled northwest along the Scioto River and then intersected the Walhonding.

Our ancestors were always in motion. Relocation was a bet on the future. For former slaves, it meant a chance to live free and raise their families on free soil. They were looking for the best opportunity to become independent and successful on their own terms. There were several ways to travel to Ohio, by canal, Lake Erie, the Ohio River, and the National Road.

The canal system was the earliest man-made way to travel from Lake Erie to the Ohio River. The canals were instituted in Ohio during the years 1820–30. The Ohio-Erie Canal was the canal that went by Columbus. There was a Columbus feeder canal that went from Lockbourne to the end, which was a dock at Mound and State Streets. At this point the feeder connected to the Scioto River just below Franklinton.

The father of Ohio's canal system was Alfred Kelly. Alfred came to Columbus from Connecticut, as many settlers did at this time. He was a lawyer and was very influential in state politics. He served in the Ohio House of Representatives in 1814. Because of his position in state politics, he was able to persuade the legislature to finance the building of canals to support trade and settlement. He was very much hands-on in supervising the building of the canals and making sure that there was always financing through government programs.

Alfred Kelly had an amazing home for the times, built in 1830. It was located on the National Road. The address was 300 E. Broad Street. The home was all stone, and the stone was brought to Columbus by flatboat. His home was down the street from Henry Miller, who owned the Miller Farm in Upper Arlington.

Home of Alfred Kelly, 330 E. Broad Street, Columbus, Ohio
(Photo courtesy of Columbus Metropolitan Library)

The home was demolished in September 1961. The stones were kept by many historical foundations, including the Western Reserve Historical Society. The Christopher Inn was built in its place. It was also demolished, in 1988. The State Employees Retirement System presently stands on Alfred Kelly's property.

Many of the pioneers who came from the East Coast, particularly from Virginia, would have traveled on the Ohio River or the National Road. The Ohio River was always a very busy, crowded waterway because it was a waterway that connected to the Mississippi River. Settlers who wanted to go to Missouri or New Orleans and points in between would take the same waterway. Barges, flatboats, keelboats, and in later years steamboats all were jockeying for a spot on the river. The Ohio River was not as wide as it is today, and this crowded environment was further hampered by the seasons. Winter caused ice jams, which stopped everything. When the Ohio River froze over, it made a popular crossing for slaves and settlers. The Ohio River is shallow in many spots. If you were not familiar with the low spots in the river, you could be stuck for days until someone could pry your boat loose from the sand. Sometimes this was the reason some of the settlers ended up in towns that they were not planning on making their last destination.

The most popular river craft was the flatboat, also called a Broadhorn. These watercrafts did not have a keel, and they were a bit clumsy to maneuver. They varied in size; they could be forty to one hundred feet in length and were usually twenty feet wide. They were affordable at $75 (equivalent to $1,045 in 2016). They carried all the household goods but also transported livestock to their home destination.

These boats were basically used for one trip. When they reached their destination, the family would disassemble the boat and use the wood to build a house or to corral their livestock. This was a great recycling effort, which was important because materials were expensive and too precious to just throw away. When you reached your destination, such as Marietta, Gallipolis, or Cincinnati, you could take the boat apart and use the wood to make a cabin. The flatboat was smart and efficient.

The beauty of the flatboat was that it had a shelter on the platform. This sheltered traveling families from the elements but also could be used for commerce. Industrious entrepreneurs could sell their wares and conduct business all along the river. Boats served as transportation for photographers and their equipment, as showboats housing entertainers, and as floating brothels. These individuals could travel down the Ohio River to the Mississippi River and to the Gulf plying their trade. The flatboat ended up being the workhorse of river travel.

Above: Flatboat (Photo courtesy of Steamboat Times, circa 1900.)

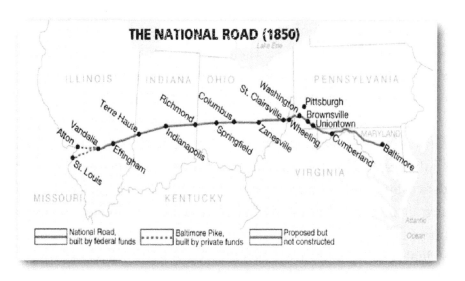

Above – Map of the National Road

Highway Road Marker

The National Road was the first highway built using federal funds. Many times you will see it referred to as the Cumberland Road or the National Pike. This thoroughfare became "Main Street" for many small towns and villages along the way. The National Road started in Cumberland, Maryland, and ended in Vandalia, Illinois. It was the main highway for travel across the Allegheny Mountains. It was important to the state because it brought commerce and settlement to the Midwest. The road expanded across Ohio, reaching 220 miles in length. The famous highway markers were placed on the north side of the road after each mile.

The National Road came through Ohio during the years 1825–38. By the time it made it to the Indiana border, transportation was still challenging. Columbus benefited from the road. The road was not paved, it was just dirt and rocks.

In some places it was a corduroy road. The corduroy road was made by laying sand covered logs together, creating a road surface. They were placed perpendicular to the travel route. It helped in some ways and hindered in others. It was difficult for horses to walk on the road due to shifting logs. However, this was a solution for roads that were impassable otherwise due to swampy low spots or excessive traffic, which damaged the road surface. This type of road was also used extensively in Europe. It was bumpy, but it worked.

The National Road changed the experience of settling in the West. It brought trade and helped farmers transport their crops for sale. It was a boon to Ohio and the growth of the state. On the previous page is a drawing of the National Road, showing the route. There are no photos of what the road looked like during the

National Road, circa 1910

time it went through Columbus. Basically, it was a dirt road, often fraught with deep, muddy ruts caused by heavy wagons. Once railroads came to take over the means of travel, many residents fought the railroad coming through their town. What they feared would happen did happen. Taverns, inns, boarding houses, and many other merchants that depended on the National Road for commerce quickly disappeared. Above is a photo of the National Road in the early twentieth century. It was difficult for all means of transportation, especially automobiles.

What was it like to travel on the National Road? The road was made of compacted gravel. Over time, traveling with heavy loads carried in Conestoga wagons left deep ruts, which made the road impassable. It was an unpredictable and rough way to travel. Walking was less jarring than riding in the wagon. Conestoga wagons were the semitrailers of the past. They carried large amounts of staple goods, such as sugar, coffee, and building materials. The prairie schooner was a smaller version of the Conestoga wagon. It was the wagon that most families used when they traveled to settle in the West.

Tollhouses were placed every twenty miles to collect funds to maintain the road. Cattle and the common two-horse buggies were charged the highest toll because they caused the most wear and tear throughout the year. Larger wagons with a wider axle, those with a width greater than six feet, could travel for free.

Pike towns were common along the way. They were budding little towns with many taverns. Taverns were the most numerous business on the National Road. In today's perspective, people think of a tavern as just a bar. But taverns in those days were much more. These establishments provided food, drink, and lodging for weary travelers. There were two types of taverns. Stagecoach taverns were for people who had money. Those accommodations were at a higher level than that of your average citizen. The wagon stand, on the other hand, was just what we would consider a quick stop. Travelers would stop to eat and stock up on provisions, and maybe stay the night in the tavern or in their wagons. They were usually located on the outskirts of town. They had the ability to provide livery for your horses.

Sleeping accommodations were not like a private hotel room. Unless you were very wealthy, you would share a bed with one or two people, often strangers. You would use a chamber pot or trek out to the bushes or the outhouse at night. Privacy was nothing that our ancestors were accustomed to or expected. Beds were dirty, full of bugs, and smelled of the many unwashed bodies of previous residents. This was a typical lifestyle for the average person in the nineteenth century and earlier.

The National Road is now Route 40, or Broad Street, in downtown Columbus. The Ohio Statehouse, Columbus Art Museum, Place Theater, and the LeVeque Tower (formerly called American Insurance Union Citadel) all are located on the original National Road.

Everyday Life

The everyday life of early pioneers throughout the country was typically the same. People of the upper class traveled differently than the middle and lower class. There were so few people in the upper class that we discuss them in this book only briefly. Being a settler was a brave and somewhat perilous life choice. In the following segment we touch upon an overview of their lives. Survival in the wilderness was much more complicated. Many settlement strategies frequently changed due to the environment. Our focus is on the everyday person struggling to make a new life in an unsettled land.

In what other ways was life meaningful in Columbus, Ohio, during the early to late nineteenth century? Life was continuously changing due to new technological advances in farming, travel, housing, and the basic upkeep of the household. Just as we have seen great changes in the twentieth century that made our lives easier, so did the pioneers benefit from new inventions in the nineteenth century. With the onset of the Industrial Revolution, rural residents left the farms for the city. Thus began the slow and steady transformation of America from an agrarian society to an industrial society. A big population shift happened, which made the city a more crowded and unsanitary place.

So what was life like for the average family? Let's start by talking about housing. Imagine yourself in the settler's shoes, there you are after you had walked from somewhere on the East

Coast or the South for weeks or months, and you had decided that this is where you were going to settle. What was next? There you were facing your new land. What did you see? The forest was very dense with very large trees and swamps, and there were no roads.

Settlers found that to get provisions they had to go to Pickaway County. They would exchange homemade baskets for necessities. Each land acquisition provided its own set of challenges. Wolves howling at night were a typical serenade.

Next, you had to build a house by yourself. You and your family slept in the wagon, under the wagon, or around the campfire. Maybe you were lucky and could board with family who had already settled there. What was your first priority? Shelter? What about food?

As a homesteader, you needed to file your claim. You couldn't build that cabin until that was settled. After that you might have wanted to think about how you were going to provide food for your family. Preparing the earth and planting crops moved to the top of the list. Many settlers lived in their wagons for much longer than they'd hoped to do so, and were still living in their wagons long after they arrived.

Now, you could build your home. First, you had to select a place that would not take on water but was near enough to a water source. Being near water was key because women and children had to fetch water from a stream or creek every day. This was a very hard task if they did not live close to a water source. People often walked miles to obtain water for everyday living. Sometimes a person used a yoke to carry two pails of water at a time. It was a happy day for everyone when a well was successfully dug and a water source was near the house. Keeping the well safe from impurities was a challenge. Many settlers placed a lid on the well to keep animals from falling in or birds resting on the ledge and fouling the well.

A flat plot of land was ideal. Then you had to clear the land. You used an axe or saw to fell each tree. Maybe you were fortunate to have a two-man saw that is, if you had someone else who was strong on the other end. Then, you had the stump to deal with. Burning it out would be the first plan of attack. Let's say that you found a friend you could make a deal with, or had many strong older sons, and jointly you could help each other. This would make the building go a lot faster. Since you were building a log structure, and logs are heavy, having someone on the other end to lift it would have been wonderful. This is why early log structures are only so high.

The log cabin was considered a temporary structure. You would choose logs that were similar in diameter but strong in substance. It did not have a foundation, which meant a dirt floor. There was one room measuring about twelve to sixteen feet, which equals about 192 square feet with one door. There were no windows, only a hole in the roof for the smoke to escape, so no chimney existed. If you were lucky enough to have a window, you were fortunate. What would you have used if you did not have glass? Pioneers would apply wax to paper or use a thin animal hide. This would just give you translucent light. Nails were not used because they were made one by one by a blacksmith and they were very expensive. Builders used a method of notching the ends and then stacking the logs. Also, they used an auger to drill holes where they could insert a peg for stability. The family would only plan to stay in this cabin three to five years, and then they would build a log home. The walls were chinked with clay mixed with straw, called daub or pieces of cloth.

When a log home was built, it was considered to be more of a permanent home. The typical log home was based on a three room plan, with a second floor and one or two chimneys. It had a wood floor. The logs were hewn and seasoned. Windows with glass made the inside more inviting. A chimney with a stone cooking hearth made the wife happier than just an open fire on an earthen floor. A shingle roof was applied. In the future, the family would cover their home with clapboard and paint it to cover up their pioneer roots. The clapboard home also showed that you did not have a history of poverty.

This log home was built by Daniel Thomas in 1844.
It was located between Olentangy River Road and Northwest Blvd.

How has the arrangement of the family changed within the household? Having a room of your own was not even thought of, and even having a bed to yourself was not common. If you had a room to yourself, you were in a privileged class. The majority of the homes that people lived in were about two hundred to five hundred square feet. These homes were called "mean" or ordinary.

Rope bed and wrench
(Photo by Plane Designs)

The word "bedroom" also had a different meaning. A bedroom was located on the first floor, whereas a bed chamber was on the second floor. Prior to 1800, people were very proud to have a bed in their home, and it was set up in the best room. It showed prosperity. After 1800, having your bed in a room where you would bring guests would have been an embarrassment. Your bed would have been a rope bed. A rope bed is made of a rectangle frame with holes or pegs, through which a rope would be woven, and the rope was then tightened at the end. This often was a two-person job. This is where the night time saying of "Sleep tight, don't let the bed bugs bite" comes from. You would tighten your rope with a tool as seen on the bed called a rope key or rope wrench, so it would not sag, and hopefully the bed bugs would not eat you up while you slept.

The mattress stuffing was made of many different materials. The sack made to contain the stuffing was called a tick. Mattress ticking as we know it today is a blue and white striped, sturdy cotton fabric. The stuffing depended on your station in life plus the availability of materials. Cornhusks, straw (not hay), cotton, wool, and feathers were the most common stuffing materials. Cornhusks crunched and poked you throughout the night. The husks made a lot of noise when you turned over. If you used a vegetation product such as straw, husks, leaves, or moss, it would break down to dust quickly, so you would have to replenish it often. Many times these stuffing materials brought naturally occurring bugs that lived off of those plants into the home, then they lived off of you. Lice and bedbugs were very common.

If you were lucky enough to have a featherbed, you were wealthy. Featherbeds took a lot of feathers to make them comfortable. These featherbeds were handed down from generation to generation because they were highly valued. Wool was resilient and held its loft over time, but like feathers it was expensive and it took a lot to fill a tick.

Many people reading this don't generally think about what we take for granted, such as running water and indoor plumbing. The "bathroom" situation varied greatly from location to location and from poverty to wealth. If you lived in a rural area, family members would relieve themselves in the bushes or the outhouse for more privacy.

The outhouse was a way to take the noxious odors of waste out of the house. The outhouse was moved as often as necessary depending on the number of people in the household. The location of the privy was important because you wanted it in a place where it would not compromise the water supply. Women would try to keep it as clean as possible by using lime as an antibacterial wash. This was a certain type of lime. It was sold as chloride of lime, which is really calcium hydrochloride. The housewife would mix one tablespoon of lime per one gallon of water. Also, she would place a scoop of lime and dump it in the hole. Once your outhouse was full, it was time to dig another hole and move the outhouse. The old hole was filled in, and as it settled, the family would continue to fill it in until it was unrecognizable. The outhouse was also used as a garbage disposal, which has brought a treasure trove of archeological items to artifact hunters today.

Ye olde chamber pot was a necessary part of living. This was a china bowl with a handle and a lid. You would keep your chamber pot under the bed or hide it in a chair or cabinet until you could take it outside when it was full. Toilet paper was not invented until 1880. Not until the mid-nineteenth century did indoor plumbing even exist, except in the most well-to do homes, and it was crude at best. There were even outhouses still in use in many areas, such as the "Blackberry Patch" and the "Bottoms" in Columbus, into the 1930s. The Blackberry Patch was located around Champion Avenue. They also existed in many other areas in Columbus.

Where did the use of the crescent moon come from? Many theories point to mythical reasons from ancient Egypt, or perhaps it was used to show which privy was the women's and which was the men's. The most plausible reason is that it was actually just a handhold to open and close the door, and for venting. It also added a bit of light. It could have been that simple.

Secrets Under the Parking Lot

Since we are talking about cleanliness, how about bathing? In today's society, we take a bath or shower every day, more or less, and smelling good is important. In the past, taking a bath was considered bad for your health. When archaeologists research historical artifacts, the items that seem to be lacking are tools necessary for cleanliness. Sometimes they have found toothbrush handles and empty bottles of perfume. Washing one's body was not a priority. Many times people would bathe in a stream, if possible.

When the biannual or quarterly bath came, the process was as follows: Set aside a half day for this family task. Find the tub and drag it into the house. Go to the well or river and carry back to the house bucket after bucket of water to heat on the stove. After you have heated one or two buckets of water, pour it into the tub and do that over and over again until it is full enough or you are tired of doing this.

By the time the tub was full, the water was just warm. The father took a bath first, and they went down the line until they got to the baby. The saying warned you "Don't throw the baby out with the bathwater." We imagine a bubbly warm bath for the baby, accidentally thrown in the air. In reality, the bathwater was muddy water, so dirty you could not find the baby in the bathwater. After you found the baby and gave the baby to a responsible person, you had to bail the water out of the tub bucket by bucket until you could drag the tub outside to dump it. Cat baths, "hillbilly baths," and bucket baths became commonplace after the introduction of the wash basin. It was thought that if you had clean hands and face, you were good to go. Personal hygiene has exponentially grown in popularity throughout time to the present day.

Commercial soap was not available for the body until the second half of the nineteenth century. Soap was used only for washing clothes and housekeeping. Soap was made from any type of melted fat, even chicken fat, and lye and water. This soap was very caustic and did not help the clothes last. I am sure it was very hard on your skin also, if you were the washer-woman. In 1791, a French chemist, Nicholas LeBlanc, came up with a formula for soap that used soda ash. In America, we get our soda ash from the vast sodium mineral beds that are located in Wyoming. When people refer to ash in soap, they are talking about making lye from wood ash. Making soap from soda ash created a much softer product.

Women of the nineteenth century were constantly at battle with filth. Rodents and insects of all types were a constant plague. Finding weevils in the cornmeal or flour you obtained through trade was not uncommon and was very frustrating. Bedbugs, cockroaches, mosquitoes, lice, and rodents were a perpetual torment. Flies were constantly circling your food. Some settlers would hang a hornet's nest in the kitchen. This strategy would keep the flies out and you also. Pioneers had to use their own ingenuity to keep all these pests at bay. Standards of house cleanliness were far below what we would consider acceptable in today's modern society. They were armed only with a homemade straw broom, a bucket, and a mop made of rags on a stick.

Woman's work was neverending. Trying to feed a family and put up enough food to get you through the winter was challenging at best. Bread was baked almost every day in cast iron Dutch oven. Meat and vegetables were boiled in heavy castiron pots. They were held above the fire by hooks that hung from a lug pole. A lug pole was a strong piece of green timber. Green wood was important because it was less of a fire hazard. In time, the iron crane replaced the lug pole. Everything was plentiful except salt, coffee, and anything else that had to travel a distance. Game was easily obtained. The Indians nearby would sell venison to the early settlers.

The cook stove was one of the first major appliances that became available to the pioneer homemaker. The cook stove made cooking much safer than hearth cooking. Open fireplace cooking was a dangerous undertaking. Fire was a constant fear for all families. Many women were badly burned or died due to their skirts catching fire. You had to make sure that your coals never turned cold, because then one of your many children would have to go to a neighbor's house and borrow a hot coal, and often the nearest neighbor was miles away. Settlers also used flint and a strike to start a fire from scratch. When the cook stove was invented, it solved many hazardous problems that faced households of the past. You could then actually stand up and cook. So as technology has progressed through time, it has shaped the means by which we feed our families and clean our homes. Home cleanliness improved with every new invention. This really was a gift to the housewife of the nineteenth century.

Churches and meetinghouses for the community also had their battles with the elements. Animals wandered through these buildings at will. They left filth and undesirable messes. Men and women frequently spit tobacco into a spittoon, and if that was not available, there was always the floor.

Early homes did not have a center hall that opened into the rest of the house unless the owner was wealthy. Basic homes opened right into the daily living space. These homes had only one or two rooms. In the northern cities, the open concept would have been considered backward. This layout was used for rural homes. It's interesting that open concept floor plans are now fashionable again, but for different reasons.

One in five homes had thirteen or more people living in it. Many times some of the residents would take in people who were not family. The schoolteacher, shoemaker, traveling craftsman, and even slaves might live in the same house. A person would have no personal space, let alone privacy. It was very uncommon for a person to live alone at this time. If you did, you were considered the "crazy old lady" at the end of the street or the old man who talked to himself.

The primary purpose of a house was shelter, the people who lived there made it a home. Small children slept three or four to a bed, often in the attic on a straw tick. During this time as in the past, many families slept in one bed. Men slept in a nightshirt, and then wore that same shirt to work the next day. Women wore a chemise, which served a purpose similar to that of the nightshirt the men wore. They also wore it during the day under their clothes. These articles served as a barrier between body sweat and outer clothing.

By 1830, the loom and the spinning wheel were abandoned, and cotton was the preferred material for clothing. Fewer women were making their own cloth at home. Wool was combined with flax to make linsey-woolsey, which was a coarse fabric, but it was used often for clothing. It was good for mattress stuffing because it would keep its loft. Wool was great because it was warm and durable, but the process was time-intensive to create garments and home goods, such as blankets. Sheep had to be sheared, and wool had to be carded and spun, scoured, dyed, and woven on a loom to make blankets, flannel, jeans, etc.

Cotton held dyes better, and it was lightweight to wear every day. A person would have two suits or dresses, two pairs of stockings, and one pair of mittens. Cotton was easier to wash and dry. People then did not have many clothes. You would have one garment in the wash and one to wear. A person would have a pair of shoes if he was lucky. Suspenders were knitted.

Shoes were not worn often. Men went barefoot or wore moccasins. If women were lucky enough to have shoes, then they only wore them on Sunday.

Not until the rotary washing machine was invented in 1858 did wash day become less laborious. Again, only persons of means owned one. Using the old washboard and a large pot in the yard or washtubs on a bench to boil and wash clothing was still the process of the day. Women had to use a plunger like tool called the "dolly stick" or otherwise referred to as a Peggy or Maiden. Clothes were patched and patched to make them last. Garments were repurposed to wear by many members of the family. This was the reality for the common, everyday citizen. Only the rich could have clothes made for them and possessed many garments for different types of social occasions. We need to remember that this was before the Industrial Revolution, and nothing was made in quantity. Fabrics from the east were expensive and totally out of reach for most settlers; thus, everything was made by hand.

Lighter fabrics made it easier for many household goods to be made in bulk. Clothing, sheets, curtains, towels, and other household goods were then made in greater numbers. Women could purchase material from general stores, and they could spend more time sewing than spinning and weaving. Living in a rural community meant many days of loneliness. Women did not have time to visit. If they did, often the next-door neighbor was miles away. Spending less time weaving material opened the door for women to become less isolated and get together to sew and quilt together. Many sewing circles and quilting bees saved women from a lonely daily existence. It was a time to talk about politics and household ideas, and just plain gossip.

When the Industrial Revolution began, the Civil War had just ended, and as a country, we were now dedicated to putting back the pieces. Economic life was deeply interwoven in the social life of the community. Settlers, as in the past, maintained a reciprocal process of helping each other by lending tools or services, and you were required to reciprocate in kind. The accounts of who owed whom were kept in their memory. In large borrowing, such as for disposable goods, butter, eggs, and chickens, the lender would keep tabs by placing marks on the barn door to keep your account. It was based on trust. Not everyone was honest. Then again, this is human nature and the problem is not exclusive to this century. The art of the swindle or con was alive and well in those days as it is in ours.

The beginning of this new phase of mechanizing how we worked started in 1865 and lasted through the twentieth century. It changed society in an entirely new direction. In the past everything was made at home, and people worked together. Taking a process from the beginning to the end many times by one person was becoming less common. Family members were now leaving home and working in the factories in the city. A basically agrarian society was now developing into an industrial economic society. Driven by volume, manufacturing of products in mass was now upon the backs of everyone employed, including children. Child labor and union development were now on the lips of the workers.

Merchants were able to gain access to imported and manufactured goods. The exchange was more sophisticated and involved an actual log book, opening up the accounting world. Women would still bring in eggs, butter, feathers, and woven goods for exchange for dry goods. Men would bargain for more masculine exchanges that would show their agricultural efforts with grains, such as oats, corn, and buckwheat. All families had a personal garden that would feed their families. An interesting fact is that tomatoes were considered ornamental. They were referred to as Jerusalem apples. Women would also trade bulk agricultural goods. If you had blacksmith skills, you would exchange iron goods, such as nails, hinges, latches, and tools. Whatever you were talented at doing, if it could produce a product for sale, then you would do that to supplement the household income. Trade, whether you bartered or provided hard currency, was the name of the game.

Light was provided by candles, firelight, and oil lamps. The use of pine knots, tallow, and lard oil lamps furnished most light. Families would have to make all the candles to provide illumination. Keeping a stash of fifty dozen or more candles was not uncommon. Until the oil lamp was introduced, life was literally pretty dark. I think Ben Franklin was correct when he said, "Early to bed, early to rise makes a man healthy, wealthy, and wise." For your everyday family, at night it was dark inside and outside the house. Not much could be accomplished, so after you worked and ate dinner, you might as well go to bed. But if you got up early and tended to your day with hard work and diligence, you could become prosperous.

Many different types of oils for illumination were used such as olive, sesame, fish, and whale oil. The demand for whale oil made whaling the fifth largest industry in America. Whale oil was expensive, so an alternative fuel was desired. The use of kerosene in 1858 became the popular and safer alternative, but it was still expensive. When we look at modern illumination, it was a luxury for most of the population.

The typical possessions of a family in mid-nineteenth entury rural Ohio included one side saddle, one trundle bed, one bedstead, bedding, one stool, one brass eight day clock, one desk, one rifle gun, horn and pouch, one looking glass, one lot of sole leather, one lot of upper leather, a shoe work bench and tools, two brooms, one rocking chair, a tea canister, three kettles, two plows, one hoe, one hammer and mallet, one lot of clothing, five chairs, one cow, one horse, a tea pot and saucers, one waffle iron, three brass candlesticks, one lot of tin ware, a coffee mill, and a Bible.

Revolutionary War Patriots and Pioneers of Perry Township, Franklin County, Ohio

Amaziah Hutchinson

Amaziah Hutchinson was an early settler coming to Perry Township from Connecticut with his brother, Daniel. They took possession of a small cabin that was enveloped by woods with no clearing. He owned property on the Scioto River on Riverside Drive. Amaziah Hutchinson, like Elijah Backus and others, came to this area from Connecticut. Worthington was also part of Perry Township and was founded and settled in by people coming from Connecticut.

Amaziah (Amasa), like his father, Captain Eleazer Hutchinson, served in the Continental Army. Amaziah was only a teenager during the war, so he served as a private. His duties most likely would have been support roles and not necessarily fighting on the front lines. It is believed he came west with a family member and located to Milton, New York. This was a common stopping point for those going west. Amaziah and his brother Daniel stayed there for a while doing odd jobs, such as farmer and tailor, and spearheaded a ferry business crossing Lake Cayuga. Amaziah was still a young man of twenty-eight years. When he was twenty-nine, he married

Elizabeth Mack, whose father also fought in the Revolutionary War. Together they had eight children, all born in New York.

The Hutchinson family finally settled in Perry Township in 1815. Since Amaziah's land pension would have been very small due to his rank of private, he obtained an unsecured title bond from Joseph Perrin. Once Amaziah built his home for his family, he put in a large orchard that served his family and the community.

Amaziah was a smart and diligent individual, and soon he became the justice of the peace of the township, known as Norwich Township at that time. Over the next ten years, the economy of America suffered. Climate changes caused it to snow on the Fourth of July, which caused massive crop failure.

When you could not pay your debt in the nineteenth century, they put you in debtor's prison. Amaziah, with others, spent time in the Franklinton Jail in 1822. He died in 1823, at the age of sixty-one.

Elizabeth and his children carried on in the home that he built stone by stone. She planted crops in the bottom land and carried on as her neighbors did. His house stayed in the family until urban crawl encroached on the idyllic homestead. The house was located between Henderson and Bethel Roads on Riverside Drive. It was razed in 2013 by a property developer who built the Berkley House Apartment Complex at that site.

Many of the settlers were related. Elizabeth Hutchinson was related to the John Davis Family. John Davis and his wife, Ann Simpson Davis, were also Revolutionary War Patriots and early settlers in Perry Township.

Below is a photo of the home Amaziah Hutchinson built in 1821 and 1822. The people in the photo are, from left to right, Laura

Hutchinson Thomas (seated), Nettie Thomas Cook (in doorway), Kate Hutchinson (seated), Jeanette Thomas Steinbower Coffman, and Sallie Thomas Artz. (Courtesy of the Dublin Historical Society)

Elijah Backus

Elijah Backus was one of the noted Revolutionary War patriots, and he owned a large section of Perry Township. On the first page of the book is a document signed by President John Adams, giving Elijah Backus, two thousand nine hundred and seventy-nine acres for his military service. He served as a corporal for the Seventh Connecticut Regiment. He was a lawyer and politician. After the war, Elijah set his sights on the Virginia landholdings to the west. In the beginning, he purchased two islands located in the Ohio River. There are numerous islands of various sizes located in this area near Parkersburg, West

Virginia. One of the islands, which Elijah purchased in 1792, was called Backus Island by him. He would have been surprised to see what drama would unfold on his land. He sold 170 acres on the northern part of the island to Harman Blennerhassett for $4,500 in 1798. This island was the place where it was thought that Aaron Burr and Harmon Blennerhassett planned treason, in 1807.[1]

Elijah stayed in the Marietta area for numerous years. He was elected to the Ohio State Senate in 1803 from Washington County, Ohio, for a two-year term.

He and his law firm partner and friend, Wyllys Stillman, purchased printing materials and started the Ohio Gazette and the Territorial and Virginia Herald newspapers. Unfortunately, the newspaper business was not for them, and the press was sold at a sheriff's sale in 1810. He relocated to Illinois and served in the court system of Ruskin, Illinois, and was judge of the Court of Claims when he died there in 1812.

What does this have to do with Perry Township? As previously stated, Elijah Backus was given extensive acreage in the US Military Lands by President John Adams for his military service.[2]

Military land warrants were decided on rank, and the amount of land you received was in correlation to that service. Elijah also purchased some land warrants from other veterans. Many veterans sold their land warrants for many different reasons. This became a very lucrative business for land jobbers and speculators. The U.S. Military District spanned many counties throughout central Ohio. The area in discussion was the southern part of the U.S. Military Tract, which bordered on the east side of the Scioto

River. The Virginia Military Lands were located on the west side of the Scioto River.

Thomas Backus, son of Elijah Backus, built a flour mill on the banks of the Scioto River in 1813 and 1814. The mill later became McCoy's Mill, Matere's Mill, and the Marble Cliff Mill. These mills operated successfully for forty-five years. There is a story connected to these mills that claimed they were near a rocky cliff that housed several dens of rattlesnakes. These rattlesnakes terrorized everyone, young and old, who came to have their corn or wheat milled.

The location of the mill was a huge convenience for farmers in the area because they could have their wheat ground there instead of taking it all the way to Chillicothe or in the later years to Franklinton. Thomas lived on part of the land warrant that was given to his father for his Revolutionary War service. This land was located in the U.S. Military Tract, and part of his many acres became Perry Township. In 1814, Thomas Backus was elected as the justice of the peace for Norwich Township, Franklin County, Ohio. Norwich Township was named by Thomas, from his early years traveling from Norwich, Connecticut, to the Ohio wilderness.

In 1820, he was the prosecuting attorney for Franklin County. Thomas Backus was a graduate of Yale College, and he was a lawyer by profession. He also followed in his father's footsteps by being politically involved in his community. He served in many capacities throughout his life. Thomas and his wife, Temperance (Lord), lived in Franklinton until 1823, when they moved to Union County, Ohio. He owned a large amount of land and was very active in the sale of real estate. On the 1842 map of Perry Township, it is referred to the Backus tract.

The Delashmutt, McCoy, and Richards Families

The Delashmutts were early settlers in Franklin County, Ohio. They first settled in Franklinton. John K. Delashmutt fought in the War of 1812 with his brother Van. Elias Nelson Delashmutt, another brother, was the first sheriff in Franklinton, Ohio. Sheriff Delashmutt died, sadly, as many of that time did, of ague (malaria), or fever. But the above fact has been clouded in a confusing oral history that stated that John and his wife, Sarah, died in 1824, while they were being treated for the cholera epidemic. The cholera epidemic hit Columbus twice in the early years of Franklin County.

The Delashmutts were also merchants in early Franklin County. They were hat makers. Here is an excerpt of a notice that was placed in the Bartgis Republican Gazette in Frederick Town, Maryland, pertaining to John Delashmutt, on October 28, 1803: "John Delashmutt, age about twenty, five feet seven-eight inches, a very impudent, ill-disposed lad, apprenticed boy to the hatter's business, has run away." It is obvious that there was family drama even in the nineteenth century.

William Trammel Delashmutt was the firstborn of John Delashmutt. William was born on July 14, 1814, and died on April 11, 1887. He finally settled in Perry Township after going west for a while. He came back and taught school in the area. He lived with his sister Ann, who married Hiram Richards. William taught his wife, Lois, as a student when she was just twelve. I am sure he saw her often since she was his brother-in law's niece. Five years later they married. Lois Smith was the daughter of Cleanthis and Ester (Richards) Smith. It is believed that she was born in Marion County, Ohio. Two years after their marriage, they moved to Perry Township, in 1844, and like many who went before them, bought property that was total wilderness. William, like his neighbor, Rudolph Phenegar, had to clear a road to the place his home was to be located and then clear the land before he could build his house.

William farmed and dealt in real estate his entire life. He gave a plot of land across from Union Cemetery on Olentangy River Road for the beginning of the Primitive Baptist Church. Once they built their meetinghouse, the congregation refused to let him attend in his farm clothes. William never went back.

Ebenezer Delashmutt originally purchased the land north of Fishinger Road in 1845. William built a beautiful residence in 1911 at 2222 Fishinger Road, Upper Arlington, which still stands today.

Both William and Lois died in Perry Township and are buried in Union Cemetery.

William Delashmutt House, photo taken by the author

This home, built by William T. Delashmutt, was the location of many Delashmutt, McCoy, and Richards family reunions. These families were all related through marriage.

Robert McCoy's name is synonymous with the formation of Franklin County throughout the nineteenth century. When Robert came to Franklin County, he first lived in Franklinton for a while prior to purchasing sixty acres of land in Perry Township in 1812. He was born in Ireland and married Miss Nancy Douglas, who was born in Scotland on Christmas Day, 1802. They came to Perry Township traveling with their two sons, James and Hugh. They had five more children while living in Columbus.

James McCoy, the eldest son of Robert, married a woman from Franklin County by the name of Ziphorah Richards. James served many years as a trustee of the township. James also started a brewery just below Olentangy Station. He ran the brewery for several years until fire ended his business.

Robert McCoy was the eldest child of James and Ziphorah. Now there were three generations of McCoys in Perry Township. He resided in the old family home. Robert obtained a common school education but had a keen sense when it came to botany. He became an avid agriculturist and was sought out for his expertise. This sense helped him in the development of his large property. His farm was composed of one hundred acres and was beautifully cultivated, representing progressive agricultural practices. The one thing the Columbus farmer had an abundance of was peaches. Also wild plums were plentiful.

Robert enlisted in the army in Ohio to serve in the Civil War. He did not see action. Robert was known among the community as a person of sterling worth and as a reliable friend in possession of a practical mind. He lived on his farm until his death.

Hiram Richards married Anna Maria Delashmutt in 1837. He was a farmer but was also active in township politics. They had a son named Julius who was born in Perry Township in 1839. Julius worked on his family farm, but after receiving a common education, he went to college at Capital University. After he left Capital, he finished his studies at the Washington Academy. He went on to be the Deputy Clerk of Courts of Franklin County for six years. Julius was admitted to the bar in 1868. Hiram and Julius owned property in Perry Township that had a common border. Hiram and his wife Anna are buried at Union Cemetery.

Hiram Richards House
Courtesy of the Columbus Metropolitan Library

The home of Hiram Richards was built between 1820 and 1850. This house is located on Riverside Drive. It is also called the Dam Keepers House.

The Walcott, Legg, and Slyh Families

All these three families had a family member who fought in the Revolutionary War. They had either inherited their property or purchased it. The reason that I am grouping these families is that since they all lived in close proximity to each other, they had a lot in common. Basically, they each had children who married into each other's family, which really made the "ties that bind." These alliances provided a strong family group that influenced each other in commerce and landownership. Walcott has various spellings, which you will see throughout this text: Walcott, Walcutt.

Jacob Slyh was an early pioneer of Perry Township. He was born in 1798 in Lancaster, Pennsylvania. His parents were Mathais and Mary Slyh, who settled in Clinton Township across the Olentangy River. Jacob and his parents traveled together to the Ohio frontier. He came to Perry Township with his wife in 1828. In 1829, he purchased 150 acres, only a few acres of which had been cleared around a small log cabin. He paid eight dollars per acre.

Jacob had the opportunity to purchase the land that became the site of the Union Depot. This land was not the best, being low, wet, and heavily forested. So he passed on that purchase. He cleared many of his properties himself with his sons, and at his death he owned seventeen hundred acres throughout Franklin County. Jacob was influential in the political arena of Franklin County. He was a justice of the peace and also served as a county commissioner from 1860 to 1863. He ran for the Twelfth Congressional

District for Franklin County. Mr. Slyh was industrious in all his endeavors and successful in their implementation. During the War of 1812, Jacob used his teams to transport guns and other armory from Harper's Ferry to Baltimore. The Delaware State Road was renamed Jacob Slyh Road. It is known now as Dodridge Road. Jacob also had considerable land holdings in Clinton Township. He cared for a beautiful orchard and a nice house. He died in 1887 at his homestead in Perry Township.

Emmaline was the daughter of Daniel Lakin, who was shown on a property list in 1872. She married Jacob Slyh on July 26, 1828, in Frederick County, Maryland.

Jacob and Emmaline had eight children: Serena Ann, Daniel Mathias, Jacob Edward, Henry T., Rebecca Ruth, Mary Elizabeth, John William, and Emmaline Harriett. Many of their children married into other noted pioneer families in the area. Jacob and his wife, Emmaline Owen Lakin, are buried in Union Cemetery.

Serena Slyh married Harrison Walcott, and an interesting twist is that Serena passed away on February 20, 1849. She was only married to Harrison for less than a year. Harrison married her sister Rebecca on October 23, 1856. It was very common for sisters or brothers to marry the spouse of the sibling that had passed away.

Daniel Slyh became a pastor and married Rose Griswold, most likely from the prominent Worthington family of Ezra Griswold. Daniel and Rose resided in Perry Township.

Jacob Slyh married Louisa Walcott, and Henry married Amelia Walcott. Amelia's father was Robert Walcott, and her mother was Susannah Legg. Mary Elizabeth married Absalom Walcott, but John William broke with tradition and married Sarah Armstrong.

William Walcott was a Revolutionary War soldier. He took part in the Battle of Stoney Point and was also at Valley Forge.

He also received a land warrant from the government in the US Military District. He came to Perry Township with his son Robert in 1814 from Virginia. They traveled through the woods by horseback carrying just what they needed. This was a common event for William since he was a veteran soldier. He was not only a farmer but also a shoemaker, a trade he plied throughout his life.

William first settled below Columbus, but he came to Perry Township after his son married Susannah Legg, who was the daughter of Elijah Legg, the head of a prominent family in the community. He was found living in Perry Township in 1830.

The 1830 census shows that Mr. Walcott was living alone at the time. He was sixty-nine, a far cry from elderly in the twenty first century. It was unusual for a single woman or man to live alone. Many times it was because they were eccentric or suffered from mental illness. Elderly persons would usually live with relatives. William Walcott was born on May 21, 1761, and died in Columbus on June 24, 1833. He is buried at Greenlawn Cemetery.

Robert Walcott came to Perry Township, bringing his father, William, and wife, Susannah, in 1828. Robert purchased 210 acres in Perry that abutted his in-law's property Robert continued living in the home place with Susannah and their eleven children. The properties he owned were west of Tremont Road, and (see the 1842 plat map) Robert and Susannah are buried in the Legg-Walcott Cemetery, which is on the corner of the Elijah Legg and Robert Walcutt farm, next to the Wellington School

Elijah Legg was born in Prince William County, Virginia, in 1765. Elijah also served in the militia from Prince William County. To receive military lands he had to serve for more than six months. He came to Ohio in 1815. Through oral history, it was said that he came across the mountains with a large wagon and a five-horse team. He settled in Chillicothe and stayed for four years. Evidently, Chillicothe was not to be his home, and he moved to Highland County. Elijah stayed there for three years. The wanderlust came upon him again, and he finally settled in Perry Township in 1822. He purchased a log home with a slate roof. In Elijah's day, Ohio was mostly wilderness, and the pioneers had to clear their own land. This was necessary due to the need for farmland for subsistence living. Elijah Legg was a long-time neighbor of Pleasant Litchford, Robert Walcott, James McCoy, and Hiram Richards. Elijah died on September 24, 1852, and is buried in the Legg-Walcott Cemetery.

Elijah's son, Thomas, was born on June 8, 1785, in Leesburg, Virginia. He was born after the Revolutionary War, but he is included in this discussion because of his relationship to his father. He followed his father as a child to many different locations, but now was the time for him to claim his own destiny.

Thomas served in the War of 1812 with the Virginia militia. He followed his father to Perry Township in 1822. Thomas and his first wife, Amelia, lived for several years with his father, and then they moved to the McCoy farm. The McCoy farm was located on the Scioto River. The Legg family stayed there for a year until he could purchase his own land, which he bought for $200. He began clearing the land he purchased, which was also dense forest.

Homesteaders had to first focus upon family. Thomas had to provide a shelter for his family. It was written that many neighbors discouraged him because he had small children at home and he had to clear the land himself. Amelia probably stayed with her in-laws with the five children. Elijah lived close enough to help.

Thomas Legg was considered to be a sanguine sort of person, and he was determined to make his farm prosperous. The first year he was able to hew and burn out enough stumps to cultivate ten acres, in which he planted corn. Those early days would have been just a day to day subsistence living. By the time Thomas reached year two, he had twenty acres under cultivation. He had eight children by his wife Amelia. She passed away on August 15, 1852. Two years later Thomas Legg married Hannah Wetherbee. All his children grew up and moved away but lived close enough for him to visit often.

Below is a photo of Lewis Legg and his family. Lewis was Thomas Legg's son.

Courtesy of the Legg Family, Patricia Graves

More than half of the people in the photo have been identified. In the back row are Effie Legg, unknown person, Amason Legg, Helen Legg Zinn, Clyde Zinn, Harvey Zinn; front row: Orrell Legg, unknown grandson, Mildred, and Lewis Legg, son of Thomas Legg.

John and Ann Simpson Davis

In the beginning, the Davises did not live in the part of Perry Township that is included in the area later known as Upper Arlington. They started their life more toward the Dublin area of the township. Their life story was incredible in the forming of our nation. They did finally build a home in Upper Arlington.

Ann is considered a heroine in the American Revolution. Yes, there were women who took part in the war against the British. She was born on December 29, 1764, in Buckingham County, Pennsylvania. It was during the years of 1777 and 1778 that Ann was drafted by George Washington to become a courier to carry messages between him and his generals. The Simpson family lived in the area between the Schuylkill and Delaware Rivers. The community weathered many hardships due to the occupation of both the British and American forces. Provisions were scarce, and both sides participated in a thriving black market. These goods were obtained under duress. This area became known for violence and danger.

George Washington and his troops were barely surviving in the brutal winter of 1779–1780. The mission was to liberate Philadelphia from the occupation of the British.

Ann was a perfect candidate to help the cause. She was only sixteen and a skillful horsewoman. Ann was well known in the area and could pass among the locals without question. She was a striking, red-haired young woman who sometimes dressed up like an old woman so she could walk among the community without notice. She hid her secret messages in grain and vegetables, sometimes in her clothes, and even in a bullet casing. When George Washington left the area, she no longer was needed as a messenger.

After the war was over, Ann was given a letter of commendation for bravery from General Washington. She was an exceptional young woman, brave and independent. She is the cousin of the mother of General Ulysses Grant. Ann married John Davis, who also worked for General Washington. Ann lived on the shores of the Scioto River for nineteen years before her death.

John Davis was the husband of Ann Simpson. During the Revolutionary and Civil Wars, if a person was drafted, he could hire or influence someone to go in his place. John Davis's father could not serve. John ended up starting his military service by being the substitute for his father. John was also a Revolutionary War hero. He fought in the Battle of Trenton and Brandywine. He was also at Valley Forge that winter when Ann Simpson was carrying messages to General Washington. William Walcott crossed paths with the pair when they were at Valley Forge, only to meet again in the future. They had many connections throughout their young lives, being known to each other when they were children. John and Ann married after the war was over and moved to Ohio in 1820. John was given a land grant in the US Military District.[4] John Davis was a Revolutionary War Patriot, and his pension papers are on file at the National Archives. John and Ann lived in Montgomery County, Maryland, until 1818.

John Davis came to this area in 1816, staying in Delaware County for two years. He finally committed to Lot 13 in the third quarter of Perry Township in 1818. As soon as he arrived, he started to build a log house. A log house had more than one room and was a definite upgrade from a log cabin. He needed to get his housing arrangements squared away prior to bringing his family. Ann was home with their eleven children, getting ready to make the journey by wagon and on foot to Ohio.

John and Ann Davis, with many of their family, are buried at Davis Cemetery on Riverside Drive. They resided in a beautiful home on the banks of the Scioto River. It was not completed until five years before his death in 1832. It stood proudly for all those years, only to be demolished in 1977 by Planned Communities, Inc. Their farm was located where Friendship Village now standing presently.

Rudolph Phenegar

Rudolph Phenegar was born in Lancaster, Pennsylvania, on September 11, 1810. He married a woman named Elizabeth Galbraith, who lived in his county. He married Elizabeth in 1836, and they had eight children. They set off for Ohio with a horse, a wagon, and as many of their household effects as they could carry. Rudolph was able to purchase land in the southern part of Perry Township. He purchased eighty acres, for which he paid $200 cash, in the U.S. Military Tract. His land was total wilderness. There were no roads and no cut trees to make his life easier. In the meantime, while he was building a cabin and clearing his land, Rudolph and his wife resided in the house of Mr. Bickett. Rudolph worked part-time on Mr. Bickett's farm. Rudolph was considered a man of high character and progressive ideals, a faithful friend, and neighbor. He was a carpenter by trade, and he helped to build many of the homes in the township. He became successful through the years by purchasing and selling real estate. Rudolph came from meager means but by diligent and forthright commitment became a successful member of the community. He held several offices of trust and strongly held to democratic principles.

Since he was an accomplished carpenter, he helped build many houses in the area. Rudolph and Elizabeth had eight children. One of those children became a noted doctor, residing on one of the properties in Perry Township once his father moved to the city.

You will notice on the 1872 map of Perry Township that there are now Galbraiths living in the area. It would seem that Elizabeth's family came to Ohio to be near her family.[5]

What was the role of Perry Township in the Civil War? First we need to discuss Ohio's role. Up till the Civil War, Ohio tended to ignore what was brewing in the political climate of the federal government. The focus of Ohio was to continue the state's development in becoming one of the most industrious states in the Union. They had agriculture, manufacturing, and a transportation infrastructure that provided fluid motion to transport goods and services to other states. The location of Ohio, bordering on the Ohio River and Lake Erie, allowed for brisk traffic through the waterways. Columbus had the railroads and the National Road, which provided access to eastern and western states.

Up until the Civil War, slavery was not permitted in Ohio. Still, federal law prohibited the harboring of slaves within their boundaries. This was problematic, since Ohio had a thriving abolitionist movement and possessed an active Underground Railroad system.

Columbus also was the location of Camp Chase, which started out as a military training facility. It was later used as a confederate prison.

William Neil came to Perry Township in 1818, which made him one of the earliest pioneers. He came from common means, but what he lacked in money he made up for in abundant drive and ideas. Billy Neil, as he was called, learned how to be a surveyor. He saw a desperate need and opportunity in transportation and knew he could fill that void. Most of the roads at this time were old Indian paths and cattle roads that were widened to make way for wagons. William was an entrepreneur. He had an innate ability to know what would be successful. Having had a vision for transportation, to help with the settling in of Central Ohio he developed a stagecoach business. This business would carry passengers, mail, and small necessities. To fill that void, he developed the first stagecoach line, which provided necessary transportation choices. Anyone who was riding a stagecoach in the 1850s was riding on one of William Neil's coaches. He was known as "the Old Stage King."

William Neil

WILLIAM NEIL.

(Photo courtesy of the Columbus Metropolitan Library)

It is believed that William paid for Pleasant Litchfords Black Law bond, which offered a way for a family of former slaves to become successful in life going forward. William saw potential in Pleasant as a master blacksmith and a desire to become a successful and active part of the community.

Robert Neil was the third person who sold Pleasant Litchford property that year, on August 19, 1846. He went into an agreement with Robert to lease the land until he could purchase it out right. He used the land for farming. Pleasant was to keep the dwelling on the property weather boarded and whitewashed. Pleasant had already obtained two parcels of land prior to the Neil agreement. This was how Pleasant built up his landholdings

William Neil and his wife, Hannah, purchased large amounts of property in Clinton Township, which was just across the Olentangy River from Perry Township. Hannah, William's wife, was very influential in the settlement of Franklin County, Ohio. To this day, there are many programs for the poor and for underprivileged persons that Hannah Neil founded. She was considered the city's "guardian angel." Hannah was one of the earliest members of the Columbus Female Benevolent Society, which became the oldest active charity in the city. This charity then became the Hannah Neil Mission and Home for the Friendless. William and Hannah Neil participated in many other philanthropic endeavors. Their generosity and caring for those who struggled in life were aboveboard. His property was located where Ohio State University now stands.

Hannah Neil Mission and Home for the Friendless
(Courtesy of the Columbus Metropolitan Library)

Two

A UNITED, NOT DIVIDED, COMMUNITY.
BLACK HISTORY IN PERRY TOWNSHIP.

The Pleasant Litchford Story Born a Slave, Died a Millionaire

In 1789, a son was born to a slave belonging to the Litchford family of Lynchburg, Campbell County, Virginia. How would it ever have been known that this child would become a guiding force for the black community in Columbus, Ohio? Pleasant Litchford, a free person of color, his wife Patience (Catherine) Fisher, and his five sons, Miles, Abraham, Elias, Frederick and Pleasant Blake, came to Ohio in 1829. His other children were Ardena, Sarah, Catherine Jane, and Mabella; all were born in Perry Township, Ohio. You will find this family under many different spelling variants of Litchford. This name was spelled Litchford, Litchferd, Latchford, Leitchford, Litchfield, and Letchford. To keep the continuity of the book, we will continue to use the spelling that Pleasant used in his will and other legal documents. Not until William H. Litchford was identified as Litchferd would that spelling be recognized on the family lineage, from the 1930s going forward.

Pleasant's family had been given their manumission papers by his master in Virginia around 1828. He was a master blacksmith by the time he left Virginia. He was probably hired out from the plantation because he did have money when he came to Ohio. He made sure that his sons had learned this trade, which they all fell back on throughout their lives. The identity of the Litchford family that owned them has not yet been determined. Once slaves were provided freedom, they had to leave the state of Virginia within a year.

Manumission papers were documents that were provided to the freed slave. Masters freed their slaves for various reasons, many of which are unknown in documents unless they were freed by probate at the death of the master or by self-purchase. It was very important for freed slaves to register these freedom papers with the Clerk of Courts office to prevent kidnapping and to protect themselves from slave catchers. Pleasant's manumission papers had not been located as of this printing and may be lost to history.

Pleasant and his family traveled over the Alleghenies, as many pioneers did, by wagon,[5] taking the National Road to Columbus from Virginia. He most likely would not have traveled on the Ohio River because even though he was a free person of color, it would have been a more dangerous route. The National Road, also called the Cumberland Road, was built from 1811 to 1834 and was the first highway in America. This was the main way to travel west for many pioneers. When they arrived in Franklin County, it was a small settlement within a forest. Franklinton was the first true settlement in the area.

It seems that Pleasant and his family arrived in Ohio about 1829. They lived for several years in the forest by what is now the area where the statehouse is located. Oral history says that Pleasant went back to Virginia to purchase his mother for $500, which is equivalent to $10,000 today, and brought her to Ohio. The family history states that she died along the route to their new home or soon after she arrived. This same story is also part of the oral history in the Depp Family but with a different family member. The Litchfords and the Depps were related, so I believe that this story may have become confused throughout the decades. Contrary to the oral history told, primary sources show a woman over fifty-five living at Pleasant's home in 1840. This most likely was Pleasant's mother. Her name and her history, including her burial place, are still unknown, but it will be assumed that she is buried in the cemetery that Pleasant set aside on his farm.[6]

In 1832, Pleasant had to pay a bond so that he could live in Ohio. He wanted to raise his children on free soil. During this period of time, the "Black Laws" existed, which meant that persons of Negro or mulatto descent had to pay a bond of $500 to prove to the community that they would not be a burden to society. They were also required to present two freeholders to sign, securing good behavior. This had to be paid to the Clerk of Court of Common Pleas of the county. The Black Law was implemented to hinder blacks from settling in Ohio. This was also to cause difficulty in economic, social, and educational progress in the black community.[7] People of color could not stay in the city limits of Columbus after dark, so they lived in the country. Henceforth, Pleasant settled in Perry Township. It is believed that Pleasant's neighbor, William Neil, paid the bond and that Pleasant indentured his son, Miles, to William to pay the debt.[8] After a couple of years, Miles ran away from Columbus after a disagreement with his father. This disagreement broke the bonds of father and son.[9] The Black Laws were repealed in 1849.

The focus of the Litchford family was to be free, educated, and devoted to their church. Many families throughout Perry Township and Columbus proper were connected to Pleasant Litchford. The Litchfords were intertwined with the Depp family of Delaware County, Ohio. Two of their children married into this family. The Goode's, Swains, and a Litchford branch of the family resided in Sellsville. All these families were connected to the antislavery movement and the Second Baptist Church or other churches that were part of the movement.

The population of the black community continued to grow throughout the nineteenth century in Perry Township. By 1860, there were 38 people of color, growing to 112 by 1900. In 1900, there were twenty-two day laborers working as "batchers," who were people who worked in mass production of some sort. My thought is that these twenty-two workers were the laborers from Sundown who worked on the Miller farm. The rest of the black population was in farming. Also, a large faction of Italian workers came upon the scene in 1900 in Perry Township to work in the quarry.

Pleasant made sure that his children were educated, so they were homeschooled. He was determined that his children had the tools to be successful in a difficult and many times unforgiving world. In 1872, Pleasant deeded a parcel of his property to the Board of Education for Perry Township for a colored school. This colored school was built at the location of the present-day Upper Arlington Senior Center.

Pleasant and his wife Catherine were devoutly religious people. They were very influential in the founding of the Second Baptist Church. Pleasant was one of the founders and an elder in this church until his death. Sometimes, Pleasant was referred to as a lay pastor during his life. At his death he was the oldest member of the original church. The original church was the AME church. The church congregation split due to differences in philosophy, and the Second Baptist Church was organized under the leadership of James Poindexter.[10] The main cause for the division was that some of the members felt that one had to become more vocal to make change. The abolishment of the institution of slavery was preached from the pulpit, and this was a common dialogue within the black churches in those days.[11]

There was also a dust-up concerning a black family that joined the church and "owned" slaves. This was not the same as white people owning slaves. Blacks owned slaves to save those people from difficult circumstances. James Poindexter was a devoted member and local preacher for seventy-eight years. James and Pleasant were good friends, working together on the antislavery movement and sharing a devotion to the church.[12]

Pleasant Litchford, James Poindexter, and their colleagues attended numerous local meetings that discussed the injustices toward the Negro citizen. They were not allowed to vote, which was one of the cornerstones of the general discussion about Negro rights and slavery issues.[13]

With the Civil War looming in the future, a large meeting was held on October 6, 1862, to endorse the Republican candidate, Abraham Lincoln. The Free Soil Party held meetings in the city, addressing the usual slavery problems.

Pleasant was considered a master blacksmith in Virginia. He taught all his sons the blacksmith trade, which all of them employed as an occupation at one time or another. It has been believed that he may have played a part in the building of our statehouse since skilled workmen were at a premium. Many sources point to this being true, but no direct source exists.

Ohio Statehouse in the early years

After several years of living in Columbus, Pleasant purchased his first plot of land from James and John Legg on May 25, 1833, for which he paid cash. He paid two dollars per acre. His second purchase was from John Walcott on November 7, 1833, for a parcel of seventy-acres. Third, he purchased land from Robert Neil, son of William Neil, on February 1, 1849. Pleasant leased land from others and also leased some of his own land as seen in a lease to James Foley in August 1846. This was the beginning of many land purchases, and at one point he held more than 227 acres. He was the 4th largest landowner in Perry Township in 1860. His holdings stretched from where the Tremont Elementary School, Upper Arlington Library, and Northam Park are located to just below the intersection of Kenny and Tremont Roads. His home and the family burial plot included the property on which the Upper Arlington High School building now stands. This was once called the Litchford Township Road.

Pleasant was a very dedicated family man. He set aside a half acre of his property, located halfway down Brandon Road between Ridgeview and Zollinger Roads in Upper Arlington, Ohio, to be his family burial plot.[15] Many nonrelatives were buried at Litchford Cemetery because people of color were not allowed to be buried in cemeteries that served the white community in this area. Perry Township was a very rural area at this time.

Catherine Litchford, Pleasant's first wife, died after 1850 and was buried in the family plot. Pleasant had nine children at the time and only two adult children living at home and one grandchild.

Pleasant married his daughter Ardena's mother-in-law Frances Evans, in 1861.[16] Frances was the mother of William Evans. William Evans died young, and his wife, Ardena, Pleasant's daughter, still kept his antislavery philosophy. Pleasant and William had a lot in common because he was also instrumental in the antislavery movement in Indiana. Pleasant was well known in Jefferson County, Indiana, in the small town of Madison. He must have spent a lot of time visiting his daughter since the newspaper states that he was well known and respected in the area.[17] Frances, Pleasant's second wife, lived for two years after they married and died in 1863. She was buried in Litchford Cemetery.

Pleasant spent the rest of the two decades working his farm, blacksmithing, and participating in the antislavery movement. He raised cattle and horses on his farm. It is believed that he worked as a blacksmith from his farm, providing metal materials for farm and home use.

He was married again, to Charlotte (Lottie) Stewart, on March 1, 1866, and they lived out his days together.[18] Charlotte was born in Washington, DC.

In 1872, Pleasant and Lottie sold a small parcel of their property to the Perry Township Trustees to build a school for colored children. Their good friend James Poindexter was on the school board at the time, and I am sure this helped to advance this transaction. The school was established where the Upper Arlington Senior Center is located today.[19]

Pleasant was well liked in the Madison, Indiana, community, which was located on the Ohio River, a perfect place for runaway slaves to cross. Pleasant died while visiting his daughter Ardena in Madison on April 6, 1879. A notice in the *Cincinnati Star* stated that Rev. Mr. Litchford, colored, aged ninety, died at Madison, Indiana.[20] He was a lay preacher and knew his Bible well. In many circles he was called Reverend. She brought her father home to Columbus to bury him on the property that he loved so much. He was placed in the family plot near his first two wives. When Pleasant died, his estate was worth $75,000 is equivalent to 1,924,282.00 in 2019.[21] Pleasant's story is about a man who was born a slave and died a millionaire. He, his wife, and his children were in bondage until he was almost forty. He was a father of five boys at this time, all of whom had been born into slavery.

When Pleasant died, he left a seven page will, which gave each of his children a part of his landholdings. He made provisions to leave acreage to his firstborn son, Miles, from whom he had been estranged for many decades. He did not know if he was alive or dead. Miles never came back to Columbus until his father had passed away. Whatever came between them was something that could never have been mended on Miles's part. The will is recorded in the Franklin County Probate Court, Record G 535, docket 9, page 408, journal 16, page 227.[22]

Pleasant Litchford's Family

Pleasant and Catherine had eleven children. Two children died in infancy, and we believe they were buried in Litchford Cemetery, since two infants were found on the exhumation inventory by Union Cemetery. In Pleasant's obituary, it states that he had seven children who lived to adulthood. In 1850, records show eight children in the Litchford household: Elias, Abraham, Frederick, Pleasant (Blake), Ardena, Sarah, Catherine Jane, and Mabella. Miles, his oldest, was living in Salt Lake City and left long before 1850, and Mabella, at this publishing, has been lost to history. So the presumption would be that she passed prior to 1878.

The Litchford family was very prosperous and helped shape the city in which they lived. Miles was Pleasant's and Catherine's firstborn. He was born prior to 1817, also into slavery under the Litchford Family of Campbell County, Virginia. Miles was about eleven years old when he came to Ohio. He also knew the trades of blacksmith and farmer.

Miles, the son that Pleasant never forgot, left Ohio for the west to make a new life. He went south and then on to the West. He became friends with a man named Green Flakes. Green was part of a group of free and enslaved blacks who were making a new life in the West. Green was living in the South at the time he met Miles. Together with the Crosby's, also free people of color, they went to Salt Lake City to come together with Brigham Young. Miles ended up settling in Salt Lake City. He became involved in mining and also invented a saw that could cut stone.[23] Miles sure had his father's tenacity to make a life worth living. His father trained him to be a blacksmith like him. This occupation served Miles well in the trade in Utah. He lived in Utah for over forty years, and he obtained great wealth from his business enterprises in the mining industry. He married a woman named Rose Crosby, daughter of the Crosby's, who traveled from Mississippi with Miles, and they had five children whom we can identify.

Miles returned to Columbus after he heard from S. W. Lakin, a neighbor nearby his family's homestead, that his father had died. Pleasant had placed in his will that Miles, if he were still alive, would receive his equal share of the land in Perry Township. If it was proven that Miles was deceased, it would go to his heirs. In 1895, Miles sold his interest in the Iron Lode Big Cottonwood Mine in Utah. He also liquidated much of his property throughout that year. Miles ended up dying around 1902, location not verified. His share of the original Pleasant Litchford land in Perry Township ended up going to Catherine Litchford Walker. (See articles on Catherine Litchford Walker.)

Elias Litchford was born into slavery in Virginia in 1817. He lived in Perry Township, his entire life. He married a woman named Lydia in 1845. In 1860, Elias showed a net worth of $1,800 in real estate that he owned in Perry Township. He owned a farm next to his brother Abraham, which was in the area of the Upper Arlington Public Library.

Abraham was also born in Virginia in 1822. He married Matilda Jane Easley. He was a farmer and property holder in Perry Township. Abraham's farm was at the location of the Tremont Elementary School. His sister Ardena owned the property adjoining her brother's. In 1860, Abraham also owned a farm that was next to his brother Elias's farm, and that farm had a net worth also of $1,800. Abraham enlisted in the Union Army Colored Troops with his brothers Frederick and Blake. Abraham was forty-four years old at the time.[24]

Blacksmiths were very important in the Civil War. They were needed to repair arms, shoe horses, make nails, forge metal tire for wagons, etc. Blacksmiths were a very important part of a unit, especially if the unit was an animal heavy unit, such as the cavalry. All the Litchford sons were blacksmiths like their father. It would be highly possible to find their participation in the war, even on a support level. Ohio was not in the thick of the war, but they did provide supplies to the troops.

After his father died, Abraham was living at 137 North Fourth Street in Columbus, between Pearl and Spring Street. He ran a livery and also plied the blacksmith trade. The census states that he was a horse doctor. Pleasant raised horses and I am sure that Abraham with decades of dealing with horses helped him gain expertise in healing them.

By the time Abraham was in his seventies, he owned the home on 173 North Fourth Street. Abraham died on Nov. 23 1900 and is buried in Greenlawn Cemetery.

Abraham's daughter, Fannie, was a schoolteacher and never married, but she owned considerable property in Upper Arlington.

In the 1930s she sold some of her property to the Arlington Ridge Realty Company. The Arlington Ridge Realty Company split the land into a subdivision, which was developed in what is known as the Brandon Heights Addition.[25]

Frederick was born in Virginia in 1827. He also owned a farm in Perry Township. He married Maria Beson on June 6, 1850. Maria, also found as Mariah, passed away in 1860 she was born in Virginia in 1830 and was buried in Litchford Cemetery. They had 4 children: Sarah, (1851), Irdenia, (1853), Frederick A. (1856) and Emma, (1859).

His second wife was Virginia. She shows up in the 1870 census. He joined the draft to be part of the Ohio troops with his brothers. He was thirty-six years old. He was also not called to fight.[26]

Frederick was a successful blacksmith in Columbus in 1870. He held real estate valued at $3,000 at this time. By 1900, Frederick sold the farm and moved in with his family within the city limits of Columbus to 215 Seventeenth Street. Frederick died on Jan.6, 1906, and is buried in Greenlawn Cemetery. Somehow, along the line, the family changed the spelling of the name to Litchferd. Many descendants of this branch of the family go by this spelling variant.

Blake was born in 1828 in Virginia. He was the last of the children born into slavery. Pleasant Blake Litchford married into the Depp family. He wedded Mary Matilda Depp, the daughter of Aurelius Depp, in Delaware County, Ohio, on August 10, 1858. Mary Matilda was born in Powhatan County, Virginia, in about 1830. Her family was also of freed slaves from Virginia. Blake enlisted in the Civil War with his brothers Abraham and Frederick in June 1863. The end of the war was still eighteen months away. The Depp family was strongly entrenched in the Underground

Railroad. This meant that the Litchfords and other people, white and black, around them were also involved in the transportation of slaves to freedom.

Hundreds of slaves passed through the safe houses at Lucy Depp Settlement, which was named after Mary Matilda's grandmother. In the 1880 census, it was recorded that Blake and his family owned a farm in Perry Township. The Litchford's and the Depp's were prosperous farmers in the area.

Ardena, also known as Diana, was born in 1830 in Perry Township. She was possibly a twin or born in January or February of that year since her sister Mabella was also born the same year. Ardena married William Evans of Madison, Indiana. William Evans was influential in the antislavery movement in southern Indiana. William was a porter for the railroad, which was an ideal job to assist families running from slavery to travel north. Madison was a very small town on the Ohio River and was a popular stop on the Underground Railroad. Pleasant and William had a lot in common, having similar beliefs and religious convictions. Pleasant spent a fair amount of time in Madison, Indiana. In his obituary, it states that he was well liked and a known person in Madison. Pleasant married Ardena's mother-in law, Frances Evans, who was a widow in her mid-forties. Frances was Pleasant's second wife. She died three years after they married and was buried in Litchford Cemetery in Columbus, Ohio.

Mabella shows up on the 1850 census but not after that. Mabella is only noted in the 1850 as Mabella and not Marabella, since we don't have any facts to dispute this name variation. We will assume at this time that she passed away, since there is no other reference to her after that time. She would have been buried at Litchford Cemetery.

Her sister Sarah was born in Perry Township in 1832. She never married but became a schoolteacher at the Loving School, which was named after the esteemed Columbus physician Dr. Sterling Loving. The Loving School was a part of the Columbus City School System in the 1870s. Black students in the City of Columbus at that time attended the Loving School. The early grades of the school were integrated. As with many children of the time, few went on to higher education. Only the wealthy children of people of color were fortunate enough to stay. Sarah must have died prior to her father's writing his will, since she was not mentioned, like her sister Mabella.

Catherine Jane married Aurelius Depp of Delaware, Ohio. Aurelius Depp was the son of Abraham and Lucy Depp. They were married in September 1858. The Lucy Depp Settlement in Delaware was named after his mother. Aurelius and his father were very important players in the Underground Railroad in Franklin and Delaware Counties.

Catherine Jane married well. Her husband, Aurelius Depp, was an educated man. He attended Oberlin College for two years not long after his arrival in Ohio at the age of twenty-two. The Depp's owned many landholdings in Franklin and Delaware County. During the Civil War, Catherine needed her family the most, as her husband fought in the Twelfth United States Colored Infantry. He was in the Battle of Nashville, in Franklin, Tennessee, and Decatur, Alabama. He was also at Camp Chase while it was a Union training facility. Once he returned from the war, he continued to be a successful farmer and stock raiser. Their most important legacy was their assistance in the Underground Railroad and the many lives they saved. The Lucy Depp Settlement was a huge turning point for many in the antislavery movement.

Secrets Under the Parking Lot

As a researcher, I analyze primary source documentation and try to come to a conclusion about Pleasant's participation in the Underground Railroad. Pleasant's farm is close to the Scioto River. Escaped slaves came to safe houses and were journeyed off to waterways. Since two of Pleasant's children married into the Depp family, it would seem strongly possible that he was part of the process. Slaves would come up the Scioto River to the Depp farm. The Scioto River at this juncture had caves and rocky overhangs where fugitive slaves could hide. The Lucy Depp settlement was an Underground Railroad stop in central Ohio. Their farm was located west of Route 33 in southern Delaware County.

A fascinating find among old deeds and plat maps was that up until 1927 or thereafter, Ridgeview Road was called Litchford Township Road. It was first noticed on the deed of Maria Litchford to her sister Fanny Litchford in 1921. Fanny then sold the property to the Arlington Ridge Realty Company in 1940. The deed stated that the township road was now Ridgeview Road. Fanny and Maria were the daughters of Frederick Litchford and the granddaughters of Pleasant.[27]

The road was renamed Guilford Road and then Ridgeview Road when they platted the land for the Brandon Addition. So what is the real story about Litchford Road? During the nineteenth century, when people resided in rural areas, many of the roads were named after the people who lived on either side. The Litchfords had large farms on both sides of what is now Ridgeview Road. Since "Litchford Road" was a township road, people of the area referred to it as Litchford Road. It even showed up on deeds and in the Columbus Phone Book in 1910.[28] This was a very common practice, naming hollows, mountains, valleys, waterway sites, and roads were landscapes distinguished by those who lived there. So, before Ridgeview Road was provided an official name, this township road was originally called Litchford Road.

Perry Township's Colored School

What a surprise I had as I was looking at a map that I have looked at for more than six months. This was a not clear notation on one of Pleasant's properties. As I dragged out the magnifying glass, I was so surprised to see that it said "Colored SH" on the 1872 plat map of Perry Township, showing a colored school.[29] This changed a lot of the perception I had about education in the black community in this rural area. This school was located where the Upper Arlington Senior Center now stands, on Litchford Road. In 1872, Pleasant Litchford sold a parcel of his land for the building of a colored schoolhouse and facilities to the Perry Township Board of Education. Pleasant and his wife Charlotte (Lottie) sold this parcel for one dollar for the public benefit of the community.[30] James Poindexter, Pleasant's long-time friend and fellow abolitionist, was on the school board. Pleasant was dedicated to making sure that the colored population was given the same chance to read and write as white children. Children had to walk through dense woods to attend school. Hopefully, the school located on Pleasant Litchford's farm helped ease the long journey for children to and from school.

Education for the colored community was very limited. The colored schools that were in existence in Franklin County were located far from the rural community. This meant long walks for children of color as they passed schools for white students. As we saw with Pleasant Litchford's commitment to education, the financial support for these schools came primarily from private funds given by the colored families and white sympathizers. Throughout this study, it appears that the white community was basically supportive of Pleasant's school, because if they were not, they would have aggressively stopped him from building a school. Because the schoolhouse was a building and not held in someone's home, we know that the black community was prosperous. The teacher would have been a person of color. Pleasant's daughter and his niece were both teachers. It is assumed that one of them was possibly one of the teachers in the school he provided.

At the State Convention of the Colored Citizens of Ohio, in 1851, James Poindexter brought to the floor that it was imperative that the colored people of the state of Ohio immediately establish schools under the Common School Laws of 1849. This brings to light how racism during this era of Ohio excluded African-American children from the public school system

Once black students were admitted to the integrated schools, this should have been a win-win all around, but it was not. The black teachers could not teach in a white school. So here you made one step forward for the students, which was hard-fought, and one step back for the black teachers.

Throughout our research we never could find the name of the school. Most likely it was just called the "colored school."

Pleasant Litchford embraced education as a way to become a successful person. His descendants became the legacy he strived for in his life. Many descendants achieved high degrees of education and social prominence. The following list shows some of the family and their academic accomplishments:

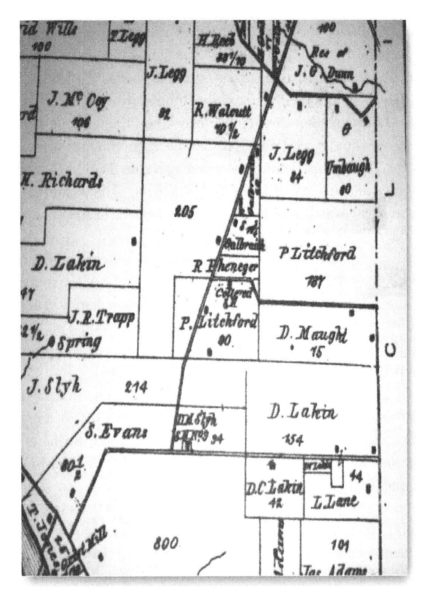

1872 Plat Map of Perry Township, Franklin Co. Ohio.
(Franklin County Engineer's Office)

Colored School shown on Litchford Township Road, or Ridgeview Road.

Edith Alicia Jones One of the first black women to graduate from Ohio State University, 1912, she received a BS in Education.

Clarence Alexander Jones He was the first black man to graduate from Ohio State University Law School, 1912. Clarence was on the Debate and Oratory Council, Hunter Law Society, Alpha Phi Alpha.

Dr. John Simmons Neurosurgeon

Neil Bryant Contractor and real estate broker

Edith Boyd Educator

William E. Hickman CEO of Free Market Global, Inc.

Timothy Breck Boyd International President of Theosophical Society.

Christine Simmons Yale Law School Graduate.

Loren Few Simmons Ohio State University Law School, 2012.

Many more descendants of Pleasant Litchford became prominent in their fields and were standard-bearers of excellence in their community.

James Poindexter

James Poindexter was a man who was born of mixed blood. He was Caucasian, African American, and Cherokee Indian. His heritage gave him compassion for all races. He apprenticed as a barber when he was only ten. He barbered throughout his life, which became a perfect occupation for obtaining information for his Underground Railroad activities.

James purchased his mother-in law's freedom for $375 from a Christian County, Kentucky plantation. She was sixty years old before she had her taste of freedom. An interesting observation is that in the 1860 census, a seventy- old black gentleman named Richard A. Poindexter was living in his home. It is believed that this was his father.

James Poindexter was the second pastor of the Second Baptist Church. He served as the pastor for forty years. He was a very talented orator and community leader, abolitionist, and civil rights activist. He was a striking figure, as he walked through the streets of Columbus, with his shoulder-length flowing white hair, silk like in quality, wearing his long minister's coat and a high beaver hat, greeting all who passed him. He was a strong force in the Columbus community.

James was a brilliant man who served many political offices including Columbus City Council. He served on the Board of Trustees at Wilberforce College, where a building is named after him on their campus. Rev. Poindexter received an honorary degree of Doctor of Divinity, from the State University of Louisville in 1887.

James Poindexter went on to become a prominent leader in the black community. He was an unfailing advocate for education. Many educational opportunities were started in the churches as the Benevolent Aid Society. He was the first person of color elected to serve on City Council. He also served on the Board of Education of the Columbus City Schools and as a trustee of the Ohio School for the Blind. Two of his granddaughters became teachers at the school. An interesting fact is that Rev. Poindexter was offered a Consulate appointment by President Rutherford B. Hayes, which he turned down. James tried for a run for the Senate and the House of Representatives on a Republican ticket, unfortunately not obtaining enough votes to get on the ballot. He then served on the Resolution Committee of the Republican Party. During this period of history, the Democratic Party was against men of color gaining the right to vote.

His most impressive social activism was formed with his wife, the "Colored Soldiers Relief Society," which provided assistance to colored soldiers who were denied support by the State of Ohio.

Rev. Poindexter's legacy still resonates in the present day. Poindexter Village was a government housing project that had 426 units for low-income residents. Aggressive plans are in the works to save two of the remaining buildings in Poindexter Village.

James Poindexter, Pleasant Litchford and other prominent black colleagues attended numerous local meetings that discussed the injustices toward Negro citizens. They were not allowed to vote, which was one of the cornerstones of the general discussion about Negro rights and slavery issues.

With the Civil War looming in the future, a large meeting was held on October 6, 1862, to endorse Republican candidate President Lincoln. The Free Soil Party held meetings in the city addressing the usual slavery problems.[31]

James Poindexter, Pleasant Litchford, J. Booker, William Ward, W. Dept. (Depp), A. M. Taylor, and N. Copeland, many of whom were barbers, were involved in the antislavery movement. Pleasant was the only non barber.

In 1840, an antislavery conference was held in Columbus, and these men were making their views known.[32] They were influential in the Underground Railroad, and they strived for the benefit of all black persons. James and his wife were very entrenched in the Underground Railroad movement. He provided teams of horses and wagons to transport slaves through the system. Here is an interesting story that was told about the Underground Railroad in Columbus. This oral history was related as follows:

James Poindexter and these other men, being all barbers, also cut white men's hair. It was a long-standing belief that people of color did not possess the ability to understand complex matters, so these white patrons felt comfortable enough to talk freely in the shop. I am sure it was quite humorous among the barbers. While the men talked, they listened, and they ran the slaves in the opposite direction from where they were looking. The ability for runaway slaves, to stay cool and calm paid off for many families traveling north. James was in an influential spot due to his location. His barbershop was located across from the statehouse. Men in government came to Poindexter's barbershop for their haircuts.

Barbershops were the "coffee houses" of the day for conversing about political matters.

The John A. Whaley Sr barbershop in the King-Lincoln neighborhood was the hub of the community. (Courtesy of the Columbus Metropolitan Library.)

Rev. James Poindexter died in February 1907 after a prolonged bout of pneumonia, with his long-time friend Dr. Sterling Loving at his side. His funeral was attended by nearly two thousand people. This was considered one of the largest funerals in Columbus.

Ohio State Journal   James Poindexter

Negro Woman Becomes Heiress
The Story of Catherine Litchford Walker

While doing research on the children of Pleasant Litchford, we came across an article on a Catherine Litchford Walker in a Salt Lake City newspaper. How was this poor woman from Salt Lake City tied to property in Perry Township? She lived all her life in Utah and most likely had never been to Ohio. This was an unbelievable story that we just had to share with you. Life is stranger than fiction. The reason that Catherine's story is documented here is that it is compelling confirmation of the determination to claim one's birthright. This following section reads like a soap opera, with twists and turns. The story could also correlate to today's world in that there is always a victim, a heroine, a scammer, poor timing, sorrow, happiness, and disappointment.

Catherine Litchford was the daughter of Miles and Rose Crosby Litchford. Miles was Pleasant's firstborn. Catherine by all accounts was part of the Mormon Church in Salt Lake City, Utah. Her father had many business dealings in the area, and Catherine had lived in Utah most of her life. She was only twenty-nine at this time. Catherine, prior to her marriage, had a child by a Swedish man named William Bergen in the year 1891. She delivered the child while living in the Salt Lake Poor House. The baby was a little girl, and she did not survive. Catherine did not have an easy life by any means.

Catherine married John Walker in 1895, and he died five years into their marriage. She had a child with her husband John but that child did not survive. There is no record other than a census notation that she had two children, and none were living in 1900. In 1905, Catherine was forty years old and destitute. She was working as a waitress and a laundress at the boarding house at 49 Franklin Alley. She lived in abject poverty with hardly a possession to her name.

Sometimes as a historian, I cannot express in my own words the actual historical record. In the case of Catherine Litchford Walker, I am going to have the record stand on its own. These documents come from different newspapers, so I apologize for any repeated information.

The following is a word for word transcript of the newspaper article written in the *Salt Lake City Herald* on November 13, 1899. The primary record reads as follows: [33]

Inherits an Estate
Joy Comes to a Poor and Needy Colored Woman
Living Now in a Hovel
Has Drained Cup of Bitter Poverty
For Weeks Chief Hilton and the Police Had Been Looking For Catherine Litchford Walker, and Yesterday She Walked into Headquarters Dazed by the News.

In a little, old, weather-beaten shack supported on its foundation only because it is wedged solid between a better building, its walls dirty and bare, its floor uncarpeted, and its furnishings consisting of a table, a wood box, a stove and two chairs, there was happiness last night.

If the place referred to ever was demonstrated as anything but an alley hovel, it may have been 54 Franklin Avenue, but no number exists now on the old door, bedaubed with paint, marked with an old latch string and ready any minute to topple off its hinges into the narrow street. A middle-aged poverty stricken colored woman lives there. She lives hand-to mouth, doing all that she can to earn bread and butter, but so poor in knowledge is she that she cannot spell her maiden name.

Has Been Searched For

Mrs. Walker is the woman for whom written inquiry was made of Chief Hilton by Clinton Graves of Columbus. A letter reached the chief requesting that an effort be made to find a woman of her name, but it did not mention her color, and little else did the writer know of her. She was a daughter of Miles Litchford, it said, who left Salt Lake in 1894–95, going to Ohio. It stated that Litchford had had some connection with mining men in Salt Lake, and that he once knew a detective named Smith who lived on Center Street, and these were the vague clues upon which Chief Hilton made an unsuccessful search for the woman. She was wanted because "her father's estate is being settled."

No Doubt of Identity

"A lady told me," she said, "that the paper said you had a letter for me." She gave her name as Catherine Walker, but it took some minutes to reach an understanding that she was Mrs. Walker for whom the town had been searched. Gradually it became clearer. She was questioned closely, but there remained no doubt that she was the one upon whom fortune had smiled, and when told of it, her face wore a look only of perplexity.

"My father dead?" she said, inquiring, "and his estate being settled? And they want me?"

It was too unnatural for the poor woman to comprehend. She simply could not realize that she was an heiress to anything.

A friend who had accompanied her to the station took the address of Graves, who is, presumably, the executor, and volunteered to attend to the business for her, after which they walked back to the Franklin Avenue hut. It was indeed a happy day, an exceptional day in her years, the sorrows of which are plainly stamped in the lines of her face.

Author's note: Catherine at this time was living in a hovel between two buildings, one of which was a boarding house for people of color. This area of Salt Lake City was in all respects a Sundown town. The only property she had was a bed, a small wood-burning stove, a stool, and a lamp. Needless to say, she was living a bare-bones subsistence life. The owners of the boarding house were Mr. and Mrs. Phelps, also free people of color. Mr. Phelps worked as a porter on the railroad, and Mrs. Ella Phelps ran the boarding house. They boarded many older black citizens there. Mrs. Phelps was definitely a person to be reckoned with. Ella had a couple of arrests that had to do with assault in the past. I know she saw an opportunity to make a bit of money by taking up Catherine's cause. Catherine could not read or write and would be considered a person in need of a guardian, and Mrs. Phelps stepped up on her behalf. She noticed the sheriff's posting in the paper looking for Catherine Walker and that she had an inheritance waiting for her in Columbus, Ohio. Why did it take so long to find her? Because law enforcement was looking for a white woman named Catherine Walker. It never occurred to the sheriff that she would be a person of color. A Negro woman an heiress?

Catherine traveled to Columbus with Mrs. Phelps and found that her farm had been sold for taxes. She decided, with Mrs. Phelps's help, to get her farm back. She purchased a tent and household goods and set it up right next to the house, in which there was a family squatting. This house was located right on Litchford Road, which is now called Ridgeview Road. She told them that they were going to take her farm over her dead body. Please read the first-hand account of her struggle to get back her land. It is much more interesting than what can be related by the author. Catherine did end up getting her land back from Charles Baldwin and his wife, who lived in Florida. That truly changed her life. She worked for her cousin, William Litchferd, at the Litchford Hotel in downtown Columbus.

So the saga continued in the *Salt Lake Herald* on January 16, 1902.[34]

Negro Woman to Get Fortune

Catherine Walker of This City is an Heiress Property at Columbus, Ohio At present she is a servant in a colored rooming house.

Living in almost abject poverty, the object of charity from her friends, Catherine Litchford Walker, an olivetinted damsel of thirty summers and heir to a fortune, ekes out an existence by drudgery in a Negro rooming house at 49 Franklin Alley.

Chief Hilton of the police force, several days ago, received a telegram from the Chief of Police of the City of Columbus, Ohio, asking that the whereabouts of a woman by the name of Catherine Walker be discovered and a statement of her present condition be sent to him. The telegram was turned over to Sergeant Burbridge, who at once instituted a search in the Negro quarters of the city for a woman bearing that name.

Secrets Under the Parking Lot

HAS MANY BEAUX

Years ago J. R. Walker, a Negro, came to this city from Columbus and was married to the girl, who is now living on prospects and receiving the attention of innumerable beaux as a consequence of her good fortune. He died shortly after the marriage and his (her) grandmother, who owns a tract of land near the city of Columbus, is now thought to have died. There are thirty-two and one-half acres in the tract, which is located within five miles of the city. Its proximity to the capital of Ohio enhances its value so that it is worth several thousand dollars.

Two years ago, a letter was received by the Walker woman from Clinton Graves, an attorney of Columbus, informing her of the financial condition of the estate and bearing the news that she would fall heir to the amount of property upon the death of her grandfather. Her guardian, Mrs. Phelps, made a trip to Columbus last August and found the old woman in a feeble condition. She was considerably over ninety years of age, and her death had been expected at any time. The telegram received by Chief Hilton was thought by those interested to mean that the old woman was dead, and that Mrs. Walker has fallen heir to the property.

NO SURPRISE TO HEIRESS

Mrs. Phelps had a power of attorney to act for her ward. In telling the story last night, she was not surprised to hear of her good fortune but stated that she had been expecting the news of the death of the old woman for several months.

"Yes, Kate, as we call her, will be rich someday," she said, "and from the reports we have received from Columbus, it is not very distant. The telegram that Chief Hilton has received inquiring about her is probably an advance announcement of her death. The old woman has been in helpless condition for a number of years, and her death has been daily expected.

"Kate has been living with me for quite a while for the simple reason that she had no place to live. The fact that she will inherit a considerable fortune has become gossip among the colored men of the city, and the attention that she has received has become a nuisance."

The Walker woman accepted the situation in a very matter of fact way and claimed that she had expected to hear the news of her grandmother's death for a number of years. They made several calls upon Chief Hilton yesterday, but he was able to offer no further information than to show the telegram. Another story appeared in the *Desert Evening News* Salt Lake City, Utah, January 16, 1902, page 5.

She is in Possession

According to a story that appears in the Ohio State Journal of Columbus, Ohio, Mrs. Catherine Walker, assisted by Mrs. Ella Phelps, both of this city, have taken forcible possession of a farm near that city, which she claims to be lawfully hers. The farm was owned by her grandfather, Pleasant Litchford, and she is now the only living heir to the same. She did not learn of that fact until about four years ago, and by that time the farm had been sold for taxes. She has been fighting for her rights ever since and has become tired of waiting for the courts to give her possession, so she has forcibly entered upon the same and is now living there in a tent and is protected by two men who guard her night and day. The journal relates the story as follows: [35]

Secrets Under the Parking Lot

THIS IS MY FARM

"This is my farm, and I am going to camp here," said Catherine Walker to Charlie Bowers yesterday.

"If you put up that tent, I will tear it down," said Mr. Bowers. "$4,400 and if you tear it down, it will be over my deadbody."

"Well, if that is the way you feel, you can put your tent there," said Bowers, pointing at a spot on the ground.

"No, I am going to put it there," she replied, pointing to a little knoll.

"This is my farm, and here I am going to stay."

And the tent went up, and Mrs. Walker stayed.

The conversation took place yesterday at a farm of thirty-two and one-half acres situated near Marble Cliff, now occupied by Charles Bowers, who holds the place as a tenant of C.W. Baldwin, the owner of the tax title.

Mrs. Ella Phelps has made four trips to this city, each time bringing the Walker woman with her. On one of these trips she was offered $1,000 for the title to the property, but she refused it.

She says she had been advised to camp on the premises and make a final and supreme test for the recovery of the farm.

With that advice in view she yesterday bought a tent, a cot and bedding, and a stove and went out to the farm and proceeded to erect the tent for her protégé on the grounds.

The tent is located a few feet from the house occupied by Mr. Bowers, and she stayed there last night. Two men have been hired to guard her, one of whom will be on duty in the daytime and the other at night.

Mrs. Phelps said that the question of the missing heir and the right to the property will now be fought to a finish. She told

Mr. Bowers yesterday that the agent of the farm, *Mr. Gugle, had told her that he (Bowers) had never paid any rent, except sixty bushels of oats, and that statement was not tended to conciliate Bowers to the landlord. Mrs. Phelps said she had been accused of fraud and everything else in this affair.

"But I'll show them whether it is fraud or not," she said emphatically.

A survey of the ground was made yesterday at Mrs. Phelps's suggestion, and the land lines correspond with the lines of the deeds and will.

Yesterday evening a warrant was sworn out before Magistrate George Lakin of Perry Township charging Mrs. Phelps with trespass, the hearing to be on Saturday morning at ten o'clock. Mrs. Phelps was not put under arrest but was notified and said she will be there. As she was the instigator of the camping, she was held accountable.

This following text is from a microfilm copy that was unfortunately stuck in the binding of the book. The reason for the question marks is that the print could not be read.

C. Walker Resorts to Strategy

Pitches Her Tent on the Contested Litchford Estate

Told the Occupant That He Would Only Tear It Down Over Her Body.

—of the law's delay Catherine Walker of Salt Lake and her able co-???? Mrs. Ella Phelps, also of Salt Lake, have taken decisive steps to retake possession of the farm near Columbus, Ohio, claimed by Mrs. Walker as her rightful heritage.

Secrets Under the Parking Lot

The women are well known in Salt Lake. Mrs. Walker earned her livelihood by doing washing. She is somewhat weak mentally, but Mrs. Phelps, the wife of a Pullman porter, and an advisor who is a match ??? man, even a lawyer.

History of the Estate

The farm consists of thirty-two and one-half owned by Pleasant Litchford, a colored man, who died over twenty years ago. He left the estate to his ten children. Nine of the ten were accounted for, but the firstborn, Miles, had left home over thirty years before. About fifteen years ago, Miles returned but remained for a short time and disappeared again. Five years ago he died in South Carolina. He left one daughter, Catherine, who has lived in Salt Lake all her life. In the meantime the last heirs have died, leaving Mrs. Walker as the sole heir. She did not become aware of her rights until four years ago, and by the time, the land was sold for taxes. It has appreciated in value and was worth fighting for. The contest has been waged in parts for years without any decision. Mrs. Walker and her friends have had a hard time to pay court costs and attorney fees, and Mrs. Phelps has made a brilliant strategical move. The incident is related in the Ohio State Journal of August 12, 1904.[36]

Men Hired as Guards

Mrs. Ella Phelps has made four trips to this city, each time bringing the Walker woman with her. On one of those trips she said she was offered ???? for the title to the property, but she refused it.

She said she has been advised to vacate the premises and make a final, supreme test for the recovery of the farm.

With that advice in view, she yesterday bought a tent, a cot and bedding, and a stove and went out to the farm for her place on the grounds. The tent is located a few feet from the house occupied by Mr. Bowers, and she stayed there last night.

Two men have been hired to guard her. One of the guards will be on duty in the daytime and the other at night.

MRS. PHELPS WILL SHOW THEM

Mrs. Phelps said that the question of the missing heir and the right to the property will now be fought to an end. She told Mr. Bowers yesterday, the agent of the farm, Mr. Gugle, told her that he (Bowers) had never paid any rent, except sixty bushels of ??? and that statement was not tended to????

Bowers to the landlord. Mrs. Phelps says she had been accused?? and everything else in this??

"I'll show them whether it is legal or not," she said emphatically. A survey of the ground was made today at the suggestion that the land lines correspond with the boundaries of the deed and will.

Saturday evening a warrant was filled out before Magistrate George ??? of Perry Township, charging Mrs. Phelps with trespass, and the hearing will be Saturday morning at 10:00 a.m. Mrs. Phelps was not put under arrest, but she was notified and says she will be there. As she was the instigator of the camping, she was held accountable.

So what happened to Catherine after all this? Did she get her farm back? The property was purchased by a couple named Charles and Rose Baldwin from Florida. The couple was gra-cious enough to sell the farm back to her in 1905 for a fair price. This is recorded in the Deed Book, Vol. 396, Page 601.[37]

Well, the drama never ended for Catherine. After she paid $275 for her farm on January 9, 1905, Ella Phelps, the person who was going to "help" her get her inheritance, bought it from her two weeks later for $50. Catherine most likely lived at her cousin's hotel so she could work nearby. Catherine was still found living in Columbus in 1906, and she was working as a domestic help. Sometime between 1907 and 1910 she went back to Salt Lake City, and she married John Patterson in May 1910. Mr. Patterson was thirty years older than she was, and he died in 1917 from cancer and alcoholism. Catherine, alone again, died at the county hospital in 1917. Her occupation was listed as janitress.

There is a moral to this story. Be wary of people who really want to help you if you are coming into money. Mrs. Phelps put up all the money to help get back Catherine's inheritance, paying for trips and materials, such as tents, etc. Mrs. Phelps knew she could scam Catherine because she was too trusting, and she was illiterate. She could not be an advocate for herself. She was able to savor her inheritance for two weeks. Very sad!

William H. Litchferd

Litchford Hotel

William H. Litchferd was another interesting descendant of Pleasant. William was born during the Civil War, in 1863. He was Pleasant's grandson. His parents were Abraham and Mary (Easley) Litchford. William spelled his last name Litchferd, which broke away from the spelling his grandfather used, Litchford. He named his hotel using the original spelling. William was a unique individual in that his nephew stated that he paid for a lot of goods and services in diamonds.

William traveled the world and owned the Litchford Hotel. The Litchford Hotel was a fancy establishment that served the black community since hotels for people of color were not readily accessible to those who could afford upscale accommodations. It was located at 90 North Fourth Street in May 1916. William wanted to provide luxurious accommodations to people of his race who had furthered the community's advancement and shown their commitment to civic improvement similar to the kind of deluxe lodging that discrimination denied them.

The hotel had fifty rooms, a dining room, a reception room, a lobby, and a grillroom. All the facilities were up-to date with the latest in decor. During the jazz era in the 1940s and 1950s, Litchford Hotel had a jazz club called Club Litchford. Nancy Wilson sang at Club Litchford when she was fifteen years old, in 1952. Many large gatherings were held at the Litchford Hotel, and it was the place to be for people of color. Many notable jazz musicians of the time played at Club Litchford, such as B.B King, Etta James, Count Basie and Louis Armstrong, to name a few. The Litchford Hotel was also known as the Litchford Cocktail Lounge.

William Litchferd's club was the place to be for up-and-coming black singers. One of those black singers was Columbus's own Nancy Wilson. Nancy Wilson graduated from West High School. When she was just a teenager, she won a talent contest that was sponsored by WTVN.

When William H. Litchferd died on July 9, 1925, he left $80,000 to help care for indigent men of all nationalities. This gift is calculated to be worth $1,001,164 dollars in 2016.[38] This gift, we are sure, resulted from the care of a unique individual who lived in the Litchford Hotel.

William Hannibal Thomas

William Hannibal Thomas while he lived at the Litchford Hotel. He was also referred to as the "Black Judas." He was the first black student admitted to Otterbein University in 1860.

William Hannibal Thomas, also called the Black Judas, was born in Pickaway County on March 4, 1843, to freed black parents. Thomas was considered one of the most reviled persons among the black community. He wrote a book called *The American Negro*. The uproar and racial tension that was caused by his book took years to calm down. William Thomas was a mulatto man who broke through the color barrier by attending Otterbein College in 1859. His attendance started a division within the school, and he withdrew. He was a religious man who felt that the blacks could reform themselves through prayer. He published a magazine called *Land and Education*. William enlisted in the 127th Colored Volunteer Infantry and rose to the rank of sergeant. In 1865, he was wounded in the arm by a gunshot, which resulted in the amputation of his right arm.

How does William Litchferd cross paths with William Thomas? During the 1930s William Litchferd met a ninety-two old veteran, impoverished in finances, suffering from dementia, and in constant pain from the wound he suffered in the war. William Litchferd took in the old man and housed, fed, and cared for him. William Thomas lived at the Litchford Hotel rent free until the end of his days. He died among friends on November 15, 1935. William Litchferd's grandfather, Pleasant, would have been proud since this was God's way to care for those who cannot care for themselves.

William H. Litchferd provided in his will for those men who were aged and infirm and had no family. He never married and had no children. He was a wealthy man, and his legacy was honorable and true.

Lucy Depp Settlement

How did this land become a very important passage for Negros coming through Ohio to Canada? In the beginning this property was part of an 889-acre parcel that was given to Joseph Sullivan in 1817 by President James Monroe for his military service. Joseph's son Lucas inherited the land and sold four hundred acres to a freed Negro from Virginia named Abraham Depp for $1,100 in 1835. Abraham and his wife, China, aka Cherry, established a stop for runaway slaves soon after they arrived. Why was this land important? It was on a waterway and had numerous hidden limestone caves where the Depp family concealed many runaway slaves. It is believed that among the hundreds of slaves that came through the Depp's land to find freedom, none returned to bondage. Slaves running from bondage would follow waterways from stop to stop to make their way north. The Lucy Depp Settlement is located in Concord Township in Delaware County, Ohio. It is near the Franklin County and Delaware County border.

This settlement was named after Lucinda, one of the daughters of Abraham and China Depp. Lucinda was also named after her grandmother Lucinda Depp, who was born in 1765 in Virginia.

How is this connected to the Litchford family? Aurelius Depp, brother to Lucy Depp, married Catherine Jane Litchford, the daughter of Pleasant Litchford. The Depp family was deeply involved in the antislavery movement, and the Depp farm was one of the stops on the Underground Railroad. It is believed that the Litchford farm was one of the stops because it was by the Scioto River, where slaves could follow the river to the Depp farm and to Canada.

Aurelius Depp, husband of Catherine Jane Litchford, attended Oberlin College. After completing his education, he returned to the family farm. Aurelius invited Dr. Samuel Whyte, also a free person of color, to join the community. Before Samuel was provided his freedom, Samuel's master made sure he had an education. He continued his education as a free man and became a respected physician and surgeon. In 1880, Dr. Whyte was one of only three doctors of color in Ohio. During the first half of the twentieth century, the farmland was turned into a place where wealthy people of color could go to their summer homes along the water.

Second Baptist Church

The Second Baptist Church was and still is the cornerstone of the black community.

The church had its beginnings as the First Baptist Church in 1824. The parishioners of color decided that they needed a church that better represented their philosophy and community needs. It started in 1834, when black parishioners decided they wanted to split from the white Baptists. They made the break from the original church and established a new charter in 1838 and 1839, which had sixteen members:

Secrets Under the Parking Lot

Ezekiel Fields, first pastor of the Second Baptist Church.

Present day Second Baptist Church. We have to remember that when this building was built, this area of Columbus was still rural. The first building was downtown, because parishioners could walk to church and it was more the center of the community.

Rev. Ezekiel Fields, Letha Fields, Miles Fields, Patsy Booker, George and Mary Butcher, Pleasant and Catherine (Litchfield) Litchford, William Gardener, Sarah Woodson, Priscilla Flood, Phoebe Randall, Shubal Fields, David and Susan Sullivan, and Susan Watson. They completed their independence on October 18, 1839. They chose Rev. Ezekiel Fields as their pastor and Pleasant Litchford as a deacon. The church was granted its independence to exist on its own on October 18, 1839.

Pastor Fields served as pastor from 1836 to 1839. He was buried in Litchford Cemetery, which was located in what is now Upper Arlington, Ohio. Many descendants of Pastor Fields still attend Second Baptist. The location of the first church was at 69 Mulberry Street, in downtown Columbus. In 1844, a new church was built at 105 East Gay Street. In 1896 the congregation moved to Ninety East Rich Street. The church stayed there until the present church, at 186 North Seventeenth Street, was constructed in 1907.

In the year of 1847, the church split due to members who were intense abolitionists. They formed the Anti-Slavery Baptist Church. The congregation of this church was active in the Underground Railroad and more militant in their beliefs. The members of both churches still maintained their close personal relationships throughout the years.

Eleven years later, in 1858, the esteemed Rev. James P. Poindexter was called to become the new pastor of the Second Baptist Church. At this time the Anti-Slavery Baptist Church was invited back into the fold of the Second Baptist Church. The members of the Second Baptist Church continued to embrace the covert manner of the anti-slavery mission. Rev. James

Poindexter was a brilliant orator and political and community activist.

Sunday school at the Second Baptist Church in the early twentieth century. (Courtesy of the Second Baptist Church)

The Second Baptist is still a vibrant and stalwart part of the community it serves. The church provides a wonderful outreach program for all.

The present spiritual leader of this fellowship is Pastor Howard Washington, who leads his flock in providing an energized congregation with an impressive legacy of pride and Christian devotion to its members and the community.

Minister Floria Washington

Three

The Unknown Legacy of Upper Arlington
Twentieth Century Reality of Perry Township

Ben and King Thompson Social Engineering

In the early twentieth century, two brothers had a vision to develop a utopian community. This community would be exclusive to certain desirable groups, which would make it economically and racially uniform.

Ben and King Thompson became real estate moguls. They followed the vision of a man named Charles F. Johnson. Charles was a large-scale real estate developer. He was also a lawyer. His business model was to develop exclusive and exclusionary communities. Ben and King embraced his business ideals and were often in business with him. Together they developed thousands of lots that were focused upon the upper and middle classes of white suburbanites. Ben worked the business end, and King was the visionary and real estate developer. They had a vision of an exclusive community that would mirror the designs of Europe, which they learned from Charles Johnson. During his lifetime

Charles was active in approximately fifty-nine subdivisions. The Upper Arlington community had roadways designed to add an ambling softness to the land. These roads served beautiful estates that would appeal to the best residents with high social standards. Ben and King placed their stamp on the new community, which reached far into the 1970s.

King Thompson was a trustee for James Miller, who owned a large farm in southern Perry Township. It had enough acreage and the desired components for the vision that Ben and King had for their community.[40] Prior to Miller's death, King had platted the first lots for the community in 1914. King Thompson was one of the executors of the estate of James Miller. They obtained the property after his death. They divided the property into four-hundred lots for sale in their new community.[41] King continued to purchase land from farmers, many of whom had received their land for their Revolutionary War service. The land had long been reported to be in the Virginia Military Tract, until primary source records were evaluated to show that the land is in the US Military Tract. The Virginia Tract starts on the west side of the Scioto River. Many landowners were early pioneers of Ohio and also served their county in the Revolutionary War.

Throughout the decades Upper Arlington grew. The population of Perry Township in 1850 was 1,119 residents. In eight years it rose by another 126 residents. By 1908 the population had grown to 1,725. The Thompsons started to plan their new community for people of distinction. They provided a community that would have exclusivity in its property owners. To make sure that desirable residents owned homes in Upper Arlington, they formed the Northwest Arlington Homeowners Association. Later, a lawsuit brought to light an ugly realization that Upper Arlington was still enforcing racially exclusive neighborhoods. It was a socially engineered community. To keep the community pure, the association called the Northwest Arlington Homeowners Association put into place a covenant to camouflage the reality that was revealed in 1970.

Northwest Arlington Homeowners Association was serving as a non-profit corporation, which served the trustees of the said corporation to exercise their personal prejudices. It was formed to administer illegal discriminatory objectives. The association granted their approval of the deed to new members that were white upon their payment of fifty dollars. These funds were to go to enhancing the community with parks and other recreational facilities. The improvements were never made.

Below is a covenant that was placed in a deed, Vol. 1579, page 53, for property owned by Albin C. Reitelbach, dated November 21, 1947. This is one of many deeds with these covenants on the books. In the book, *Planning For The Private Interest* by Patricia Burgess, she notes how long these covenants were to be in effect, 1999.

Below is a covenant from a 1948 deed. To find a possible covenant on your property you must go back to the original purchase of the land.

Fifth: That, until the 1st day of January, A. D. 1999, said premises, or any part thereof, shall not be sold, leased, mortgaged, pledged, given or otherwise disposed of to, or owned, used or occupied by, any person or organization of persons in whole or in part of the Negro race or blood, and this restriction shall be a condition and covenant running with the land, for the benefit of any present or subsequent owner of other premises shown on said plat; provided, that nothing herein shall prohibit a person, while occupying said premises in compliance with this restriction, from employing as a servant a person not of the white race.

Below is a more readable transcription of the above text.

Fifth: That, until the 1st day of January, A.D. 1999, said premises, or any part thereof, shall not be sold, leased, mortgaged, pledged, given or otherwise disposed of to, or owned, used or occupied by, any person or organization of persons in whole or in part of the Negro race or blood, and this restriction shall be a condition and covenant running with the land, for the benefit of any present or subsequent owner of other premises shown on said plat; provided, that nothing herein shall prohibit a person, while occupying said premises in compliance with this restriction, from employing as a servant a person not of the white race.

If you were a person of color, you could only live or be in Perry Township if you worked for a white family. Racism started to grow after 1913.

How would King Thompson keep certain "undesirables" out of Upper Arlington? He started by placing covenants in deeds with restrictions to ownership. This went along socio-economic and racial lines. After 1948, these restrictions were no longer considered legally enforceable. He decided to side-step the law by requiring membership in the civic association as a condition of ownership. Potential homeowners had to gain approval from the association before they could purchase their property. The association had the right of first refusal on all property. This held true for the following lawsuit.

The covenant below was Kim Starr's (co-researcher of this book) mother's property in Upper Arlington, Ohio.[40]

As you can see, she was approved by the Northwest Arlington Homeowners Association and was allowed to purchase her property.

Secrets Under the Parking Lot

> Office, Franklin County, Ohio.
> At a special meeting of the Board of Trustees of the Northwest Arlington Association, held on the 16th day of December, 1963, Leah Shoemaker was duly elected to membership in the Northwest Arlington Association. The offer of purchase submitted to said association under the provisions of Article IV of the restrictive deed from Northwest Arlington Association to King G. Thompson, recorded in D. B. 1505, page 57, Recorder's Office, Franklin County, Ohio, was declined and the sale to Leah Shoemaker was approved by the Northwest Arlington Association.
> Last Transfer: Deed Record Volume 2433, Page 444.
> By /s/ John H. Page, Secretary

On March 3, 1971, a complaint was filed with the Franklin County Court of Common Pleas. The case was filed by the neighbors, Mr. and Mrs. William Anderson, Mr. and Mrs. Edwin Ambrose, and Mr. Alfred Ashley, to show that the Northwest Homeowners Association was a discriminatory body. The suit states that John H. Pace, President of King Thompson Realty, trustee of the Northwest Arlington Homeowners Association, and chairman of the Ohio Real Estate Commission, and the trustees, H.W. Brinker, Ken Fishel, George Frost, and William Yeager, were the defendants. The claim is that the above members willfully participated in, approved, and were beneficiaries of placing covenants in the deeds to Upper Arlington properties. The requirement in the covenant is that the homebuyer makes an application and pays fifty dollars to become a member of the Northwest Arlington Homeowners Association. Upon their acceptance, they would be provided with a certificate of membership.[42]

The property in the lawsuit was in the Canterbury area, and a previous deed showed that the covenant stated that until January 1, 1999, anyone of the Negro race or blood was restricted from purchasing property. They could occupy a residence in a white household if they were employed as a servant. (See the appendix for primary source records.)

Alfred Ashley, an African-American man, paid the full price of $63,500 for a home at 2760 Leeds Road in the Canterbury Place Addition in 1970. The association executed its option under a restrictive deed covenant. The covenant was considered unenforceable in a decision that was handed down by the US Supreme Court in *Shelley v. Kraemer*, 334 US 1, dated May 3, 1948. To view this case in its entirety it is filed in the Franklin County Court of Common Pleas, case number 243,983, Alfred C. Ashley, et al vs. John H Pace, et al, 1971.

In a landmark Supreme Court case, *Shelley v. Kraemer* (1948), the court held that lower courts could not enforce racial covenants. In this case, it was the exclusion of Negro and Mongolian race. The court stated that if a court enforced the restrictive covenants, then it became invalid under the Fourteenth Amendment. The Fourteenth Amendment of the Constitution guarantees all citizens equal rights under the law. No court, state or local, can affirm a legal right to practice racial discrimination.

It was found that the Northwest Arlington Homeowners Association for twenty-two years was operating as a nonprofit organization and that it was used by the defendants to discharge their private prejudices.

The association never called a meeting of the board, which failed to inform their members of the practice. The association had them return the membership fees that were collected to help the community, which was never done. The court immediately disbanded them due to unfair housing and discrimination practices. The restrictive covenants are in violation of 4112.02 of the Ohio Revised Code.[43]

Sundown Town

While doing my research I ran across the name Sundown Town in the book *History of Upper Arlington*. On page sixty-six, the book talks about how James Miller hired men living at Sundown.[44] This statement is confusing in that Sundown Town was the white community. I searched everywhere to find a town called Sundown. Sundown was not a real town, as the article implies, but a community that kept out African Americans and other racial or religious groups. These towns are also known as "sunset towns" or "gray towns." Many towns had signs that stated, "Nigger, Don't Let the Sun Go Down in Our Town." Black citizens were not allowed to be in the white part of town after sundown. In Upper Arlington, blacks lived in the area of the corner of North Star Road and Northwest Boulevard.

As Upper Arlington's suburbs expanded, the practice of using covenants was used to eliminate original black residents who lived there before the incorporation was in effect.

This discrimination was not only focused upon the black community, but it also included Native Americans, Chinese, and Jews, Italians and Irish.

Sundown towns were not exclusive to this area. Thousands of Sundown towns existed throughout this country. Waverly, Ohio, was the first Sundown town that existed prior to the Civil War.

Prior to the Civil Rights Act of 1965, Negros would use a book called the *Negro Motorist Green Book* to steer them away from these troublesome areas. Many strategies were used to prevent people of color from settling in white neighborhoods. An all-white neighborhood was a symbol of prestige.[45]

There were some establishments that black travelers could safely patronize without hassle, in Columbus.

Diane Kelly Runyon and Kim Shoemaker Starr

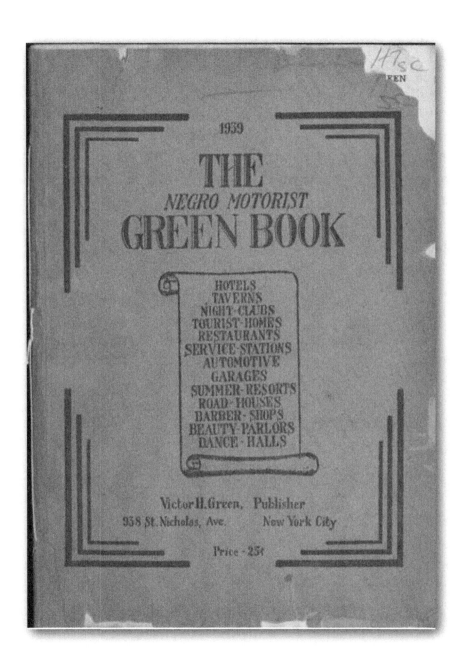

When you look back at the time in history when Upper Arlington was formed and the people who were involved in the creation of this neighborhood, you see the desire to exclude certain races and ethnic groups was in keeping with a national exclusionary dialogue that still reverberates in today's society.

The research shows that James Miller and the Thompson brothers had very strong feelings concerning excluding blacks and Jews from their community.

Nationwide, communities excluded African Americans, Jews, Native Americans, Japanese, Chinese, and Hispanics. This is the ugly truth of America in the twentieth, and to a lesser extent, the twenty-first century

Litchford Cemetery Relocated

How were black citizens treated in death? Their families found little resources to bury their loved ones. In one reference, it was stated that as for the "North Graveyard" which was opened in 1841, the Negro population would be treated in the same manner as strangers. In 1841, the Columbus City Council decided that an order be placed that the decision of black burial would come under the direction of the North Sexton. The order denied purchase of a burial plot by black residents in a white cemetery but also denied them to purchase land for a family cemetery. Families were forced to purchase a single burial plot in sections for paupers and it was always in a place that was undesirable.

In 1849, a group of black citizens of Columbus got together and established their own graveyard, which was located in Franklin Township. An agreement was settled upon by Henry Briggs, to sell a four acre tract to David Sullivan. David was a forty eight year old black shoemaker from Virginia. He resided in the south side of Columbus. The cemetery was located close to the southern end of Greenlawn Cemetery. The cemetery shows up on the 1856 and 1872 plat maps and it is identified as "Colored Graveyard."

In 1885, the "Colored Cemetery" was moved to Section 27 at the Greenlawn Cemetery. In 1885, this plot of land for burials of black residents was located as far back in the cemetery as possible, up again the fence. Not desirable by any means.

Why will the Litchford Cemetery become even more important to the black community? It was one of the only cemeteries, even though it was a private cemetery that welcomed black families without duress. Pleasant Litchford was a community man, very religious and was a friend to all. Many souls were buried in his family cemetery, who were not family members, such as Ezekiel Fields, the first pastor of the Second Baptist Church. A familiar practice by the black community of the nineteenth century and earlier was not to spend money on elaborate markers, but to use wood markers or shells to mark the grave. This was to ensure that there would always be a place of rest for all and that kinfolk could be buried together. Family members would not be located in random single plots throughout the city.[46]

The Upper Arlington Board of Education purchased the property on Ridgeview Road for the building of a new high school. A lawsuit was filed by Pleasant Litchford's heirs to protect and preserve the Litchford Cemetery. The board would be responsible for any expenses incurred in the removal of the bodies from the cemetery and in their reinterment in an appropriate location.[47]

Litchford Cemetery was located on Pleasant Litchford's original farm, which bordered Brandon and Ridgeview Roads.

Secrets Under the Parking Lot

Approximately in the middle of the parking lot of the Upper Arlington High School is the location of Litchford Cemetery.[48] This cemetery was the Litchford family burial site, where family, friends, and neighbors were interred for a century. It was started in 1830. The last burial that we have found with primary sources was an interment in 1925.

The Upper Arlington Board of Education purchased the land and was given the task to relocate the deceased. Twenty- graves were moved to Union Cemetery, and a few went to Greenlawn Cemetery. In the inventory of the graves that went to Union there were a few unnamed infants and a person in a uniform.[49] The Board of Education set aside funds of $5,000 to move the cemetery. These funds were to move ten graves, but on exhumation they had found twenty-seven graves.[50]

The Litchford Cemetery is half acre, and it is strongly believed that more burials are still there. The Board of Education hired Surveyor Harry L. Greene to execute a survey of the cemetery.[51,52] He noted on the survey, which was also verified by a photo, that headstones were shown on the survey but did not go to Union Cemetery.[53] The question remains: Where did the grave markers of this family go? Four of the descendants had their loved ones moved to Greenlawn Cemetery. The headstone of Ezekiel Fields ended up in the hands of his gt, gt, grand, nephew. He donated the headstone to the Second Baptist Church and it now resides in their prayer garden at the church.

The Board of Education, according to the minutes of a September 20, 1955, meeting, gave the authorization to remove the bodies from the "Litchford Private Cemetery."[55] Documents referred to the resubmitting of the proposal, stating that there were now ten to fourteen bodies to be removed. All parties had no idea how many bodies had been interred there, because the methods we use today to locate burials, such as ground penetrating radar, had not been invented at the time of the exhumation.

It is strongly believed that there are still remains left because, during the nineteenth century blacks had few options for burial plots. Many cemeteries would not inter people of color. Pleasant opened his family plot for anyone in the black community who needed a respectful burial for a family member. It is strongly believed that there are more burials that were not removed for several reasons.

1. They ran out of allocated funds. Remember they were only taking out ten bodies.
2. In 1955, they thought that the bodies were buried in a row. They were unaware that in family cemeteries burials were not necessarily done in rows.
3. Due to the racism of the mid-twentieth century, care and respect was not taken in exhuming the entire cemetery. Now that we have new technological advances, caskets, especially a Fisk Casket would be easily found.

It is believed that Pleasant Litchford and his second wife Frances were buried in Fisk caskets, which were very expensive. It is hard to conceive that someone buried in a Fisk would not have a grave marker. The Fisk caskets are extremely heavy and hard to remove, so a crane has to be used for exhumation. Through much discussion with other historians, we believe that the C.W. Bryant Company would have been one of a few places that would have possessed a crane to assist with the removal of these caskets. C.W. Bryant's wife, Mariah, was a grand-daughter of Pleasant Litchford. As to the account of Billy Martin, gravedigger, he thought that they placed a chain on the backhoe they were using, and removed the caskets.

Over a three-day period, all the remains that were removed from the Litchford Cemetery were located in a large expanse of green space at Union Cemetery. There are no markers or monuments to show that anyone is buried there. It is very sad that pioneers of Perry Township could be forgotten in this manner. One of the graves that is noted in the inventory contained a person in a uniform.[56]

As they look for equality in life they should have equality in death.

Marker for Edon Swain—died July 30, 1878.
Maria L. Litchford—died April 2, 1863.
Catherine Litchford—died December 23, 1889.
Frances Litchford—died April 29, 1865.

The following persons have been identified by primary sources that were buried in Litchford Cemetery. They are not all accounted for because there were people buried in Litchford Cemetery who weren't related to the Litchfords.

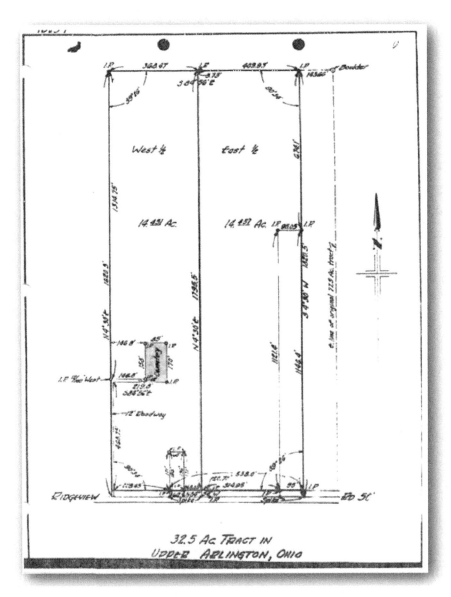

Plat map of the Litchford property noting the location of the family cemetery at the site of the Upper Arlington High School.[57]

The last burial that we can identify at this time was that of Grant Litchford, in 1925.

The following people have been identified by primary source documentation.

James Litchford
Frederick A. Litchford
Susan Litchford
Eugene Litchford
Edon Swain
Pleasant Litchford
Maria Litchford
Catherine Litchford
Frances Litchford
Ezekiel Fields, second pastor of the Second Baptist Church
Wilbur Jones Jr.
Pleasant Litchford Jr.
Carrie Litchford
Unidentified infant 1
Unidentified infant 2

The following people are not confirmed with a primary source to be interred in the Litchford Family Cemetery but are believed to be there:

Elias Litchford
Lydia Litchford (Elias's wife)

Mabella Litchford

Sarah Litchford, daughter of Frederick Litchford Mariah Litchford, wife of Frederick Litchford

During the last half of the nineteenth century, the cost of a standard wood casket was approximately $2 to $3. When Litchford Cemetery was moved, two Fisk CASKETS were found. A Fisk CASKET was made of cast iron and possessed a viewing window that was covered with a metal plate. Two of these rare caskets were found in Litchford Cemetery. A Fisk CASKET cost $100 in 1880. The last known Fisk CASKET was found in the basement of a funeral home in Manhattan. It sold for $75,000 for a 2013 burial.

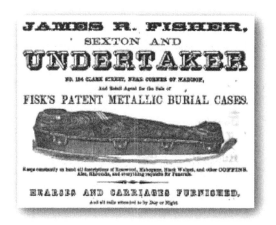 

Fisk Burial Case, made of cast iron and weighs 300lbs.

Litchford Cemetery was the only cemetery in Perry Township for people of color in Franklin County. This does not include the many private family plots throughout the township. Pleasant Litchford had a half- acre burial site carved from his farm, and many people of color who lived near him were also buried there. Ezekiel Fields, first pastor of the Second Baptist Church, was originally interred there. Pleasant lived on this farm from 1833 until his death in 1878. The property has been in the hands of the family into the mid-twentieth century. The records of the reinterment to Union Cemetery located on Olentangy River Road in Columbus, Ohio, are included in this publication. When the cemetery was moved to Union Cemetery, none of the headstones were moved with the bodies. A survey map that was commissioned by the Upper Arlington Board of Education showed the markers that still existed.[58] The locations of these markers are unknown at the time of this writing. All of the bodies that were transferred to Union Cemetery rest in an unmarked field in the back of the property, lost to history until now.

Billy Martin with the authors, Kim Shoemaker Starr and Diane Kelly Runyon Kelly Runyon at the Rutherford Funeral Home, 2015

2017 Upper Arlington Board of Education

We have been very privileged to work with the Superintendent of Upper Arlington Public Schools, Paul Imhoff, Karen Truitt and Chris Potts. John Schweikart, archaeologist, with the Ohio Historical Society. The Board of Education is committed to make this wrong right. To date, an archaeological survey has been done on the property where the "colored school" was once located. During this assessment a blue bead, see below, was found. This bead has been evaluated by the Ohio Historical Society experts and found that this bead was identical to beads found in the south connected to the slave trade. This particular bead was handed down from mother to daughter through the maternal line.

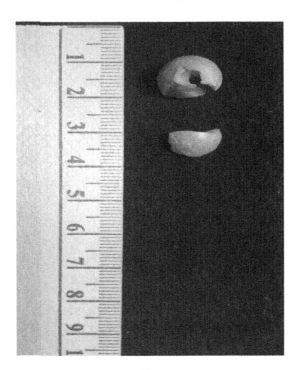

138

DNA has become a valuable tool in genealogical and archaeological research. One of the ancestors did a DNA test which verified many hypotheses. He also took the African American DNA test that was developed by a former Ohio State University geneticist, Dr Rick Kittles. Dr Kittles provided a test that can pinpoint through your DNA what tribe that your ancestors came from. We had the gt, gt, gt, grandson of Pleasant Litchford take this test and the findings were remarkable.

He hailed from the Tikar tribe in Cameroon. By studying the history of the Tikar people it is known that they were enslaved and taken to Virginia. From the genealogical record, this is where Pleasant Litchford and his ancestors possibly first landed in North America. It is amazing what science can do to tie together the missing pieces of history and provide clarity to the unknown story of the past.

Pleasant Litchford's Landholdings

Seventy-seven and one-half acres purchased from John M. Walcott on November 17, 1833 (Record Book 11, page 464).

Sixty acres, more or less, purchased from James and John Legg and wife by deed on May 25, 1835 (Deed Book 14, pages 85 and 86).

William Neil leased unknown amounts of farmland to Pleasant Litchford for farming purposes on August 19, 1846.

Ninety acres purchased from Robert Neil on February 1, 1849 (Deed Book 39, page 156).

Sources and Citations

1. "Biographical Sketch of Herman Blennerhassett and Mrs. Margaret Blennerhassett". The American Review 7 no. 4 (April 1848): 368- 84. Accessed March 14, 2016. http//ebooks.library.cornell.edu.

2. US National Archives, Washington. Office of the Adjunct General. Land Grant. Washington, DC.

3. Lisa Tendrich Frank, ed., *An Encyclopedia of American Women at War: From the Home Front to the Battlefields* (Santa Barbara, CA: ABC- CLO LLC Publishing, 2013), 180.

4. *Compiled Service Records of Soldiers Who Served in the American Army during the Revolutionary War,* Fold 3 image/15210892.

5. *A Centennial Biographical History of the City of Columbus and Franklin County* (Chicago, IL: Lewis Publishing Co., 1901), 840.

6. *History of Franklin County Pickaway Counties, Ohio* (Columbus, OH: William Bros, 1880), 379.

7. Stephen Middleton, *The Black Laws: Race and the Legal Process in Early Ohio* (Athens, OH: Ohio University Press, 2005), 1.

8. Nimrod B. Allen, John Simpson, and A. J. Worsham, *Advancement: Negros' Contribution in Franklin County 1803–1953* Columbus, Ohio Ball Press, 1954), 6.

9. Ibid., 15.

10. Rayford W. Logan and Michael R. Winston, eds., *Dictionary of American Negro Biography* (New York: W. W. Norton, 1982), accessed June 6, 2016, www.blackpast.org

11. Ibid.

12. Ibid.

13. "Underground Railroad—Reverse Black Conductors of Columbus," The Ohio Statehouse Capital Square Review and Advisory Board, 2015. Pg. 66

14. Nimrod B. Allen, John Simpson, and A. J. Worsham, *Advancement: Negros' Contribution in Franklin County 1803–1953* Columbus, Ohio Ball Press, 1954), 6.

15. "After Fifty Three Years," *The Marion Star*, June 6, 1893, 1; accessed May 24, 2015, https://www.newspapers.com/.

16. Litchford-Evans Marriage, November 8, 1861, Jefferson County, Indiana, Marriage Records 1858–1868, Microfilm Roll #4.

17. "Death of Pioneer," *Ohio State Journal*, April 16, 1879, 1.

18. Litchford-Stewart Marriage, March 1, 1866, Franklin County, Ohio, Marriage Records 1789–2013, Image 178.

19. Deed from Pleasant Litchford to the Board of Education, Franklin County Deed Records, Franklin County Probate Court, Columbus, Ohio, July 27, 1869.

20. "Death of a Pioneer," *Ohio State Journal*, April 16, 1879, 1.

21. "After Fifty Three Years," *The Marion Star*, June 6, 1893, 1, accessed May 24, 2015.

22. Will of Pleasant Litchford, April 15, 1879. Franklin County Probate Court, Columbus, Ohio, Will Book G–H, 1875–1882

23. J. A. Stapley, "In My Father's House Are Many Mansions," Green Flake's Legacy of Faith, accessed February 1, 2016. http://history.lds.org

24. US Civil War Draft Registration Records, 1863–1865 Enlistments for Perry Township, Franklin County, Ohio, June 1863, National Archives, Washington, DC.

25. Warranty Deed, Vol. 695, p. 266, Mary Litchford to Fannie Litchford, February 23, 1921, Franklin County Probate Court, Columbus, Ohio.

26. *History of Upper Arlington*, Upper Arlington Historical Society, 1977.

27. Warranty Deed, Vol. 695, p. 266, Mary Litchford to Fannie Litchford, February 23, 1921, Franklin County Probate Court, Columbus, Ohio.

28. Columbus Citizens Telephone Company, Telephone Directory, December 1910, Ohio Historical Society, Columbus, Ohio.

29. Map of 32.5-tract in Upper Arlington, Ohio, n.d., In Franklin County Engineer's Office. 2016.

30. Deed from Pleasant Litchford to the Board of Education, Franklin County Deed Records, Franklin County Probate Court, Columbus, Ohio, July 27, 1869.

31. "Underground Railroad—Reverse Black Conductors of Columbus," The Ohio Statehouse Capital Square Review and Advisory Board, 2015.

32. "Convention of Colored Citizens," *The North Star* December 15, 1848.

33. "Inherits and Estate", *Salt Lake City Herald*, November 13, 1899.

34. "Negro Woman to Get Fortune," *The Salt Lake Herald* January 16, 1902, 5.

35. "She Is in Possession," *Desert Evening News*, August 24, 1904, accessed May 20, 2015.

36. "C.Walker Resorts to Strategy," *The Salt Lake Tribune* August 24, 1904, 9.

37. Deed transfer, Baldwin to Catherine Walker, n.d., Franklin County, Ohio, Deeds, accessed 2016, http://recorder.franklincountyohio.gov/.

38. R. Barrett, n.d., Postcard from Columbus, Litchford Hotel, Columbus Dispatch.

39. "Leaves $80,000 Fund," *The Circleville Herald*, November 20, 1926, 6.

40. Digital image, n.d., Franklin County, Ohio, Deeds, Franklin County Recorder's Office, n.p., http://recorder.franklincountyohio.gov/2016.

41. P. Burgess, *Planning for the Private Interest: Land Use Controls and Residential Patterns in Columbus, Ohio, 1900–1970* (Columbus, OH: Ohio State University Press, 1994), 57.

42. "A Case of Race," (blog), October 19, 2011, accessed May 15, 2015, www.unshovelingthepast.com.

43. United States Supreme Court, *Shelley v. Kraemer* 334 U.S. 1, (May 3, 1948).

44. M. G. Sayer, ed., *History of Upper Arlington, A Suburb of Columbus, Ohio* (Upper Arlington, OH: Upper Arlington Historical Society, 1977).

45. *The Negro Motorist Green Book*, 1949, http://www.autolife.umd.umich.edu/Race/R_Casestudy/Negro_motorist_green_bk.htm.

46. General Ordinances of the City of Columbus in force January 1st 1882 (Columbus, OH: Gazette Printing and Publishing, 1882).

47. Minutes of the Board of Education of the Upper Arlington City School District, No. 192745 (Franklin County Common Pleas) (Dist. file), Vol. 1904, 623.

48. Map of 32.5-tract in Upper Arlington, Ohio, Franklin County Engineer's Office.

49. Union Cemetery Records, 1955, unpublished. Columbus, Ohio.

50. Ibid.

51. Harry, L. Greene, "Grave and marker location, Ridgeview Rd," December 16, 1955. Upper Arlington Board of Education.

52. Ibid

53. Ibid

54. " Moving Graveyard School Board's Job," Columbus Dispatch, August 21, 1995, 3D

55. Board of Education Minutes, Upper Arlington Board of Education, December 16, 1955, 97

56. Union Cemetery Records, 1955, unpublished.

57. Harry, L. Greene, "Grave and marker location, Ridgeview Rd," December 16, 1955. Upper Arlington Board of Education.

58. Ibid

Bibliography

Ballagh, James. *History of Slavery in Virginia*, Vol. 24. New York: John Hopkins Press.,1902.

Burgess, Patricia. *Planning for the Private Interest*. Columbus: Ohio State University Press, 1994.

Cayton, Andrew R. L., and Stuart D. Hobbs. *The Center of a Great Empire: The Ohio Country in the Early American Republic* Columbus, OH: Ohio University Press, 2005.

Commitment: Fatherhood in Black America Columbia, MO: University of Missouri Press, 1998.

LaRoche, Cheryl Janifer. Free Black Communities and the Underground Railroad: The Geography of Resistance. University of Illinois Press, 2013

Gray, John. *A Long Look Back: A History and Genealogy of Clinton and Perry Townships, Franklin County, Ohio* Rev John Gray Publishing, Grove City, Ohio1938.

Griffler, Keith P. *Front Line of Freedom: African Americans and the Forging of the Underground Railroad in the Ohio Valley* Lexington: University Press of Kentucky, 2010.

Heiser, Alta. Harvey *West to Ohio*. Yellow Springs, OH: Antioch Press, 1955.

Historic Columbus: A Bicentennial History. Edward Lentz- Historical Publishing Network-2011

Hooper, Osman Castle. *History of the City of Columbus, Ohio: From the Founding of Franklinton in 1797, through the World War Period, to the Year* 1920. Columbus: Memorial Pub., 1920

History of Franklin and Pickaway Counties, Ohio, with Illus. and Biographical Sketches, Some of the Prominent Men and Pioneers Cleveland: William Bros, 1880.

History of Franklin County: A Collection of Reminiscences of the Early Settlement of the county, William Martin – Follett Foster - 1961

Hunt, Douglas R. *The Ohio Frontier, Crucible of the Old Northwest, 1720–1830* Bloomington: Indiana University Press, 1996.

Jones, Mary Ellen. *Daily Life on the Nineteenth-Century American Frontier* Westport, CT: Greenwood Press, 1998.

Kern, Kevin F., and Gregory S. Wilson. *Ohio: A History of the Buckeye State.* 2013

Larkin, Jack. *Reshaping Everyday Life, 1790–1840.* New York: Harper and Row, 1988.

Larkin, Jack. *Where We Lived: Discovering the Places We Once Called Home.* Newtown, CT: Taunton Press, 2006.

Lee, Alfred E. *History of the City of Columbus, Capital of Ohio* New York: W.W. Munsell & Co., 1892.

Lehosit, Sean V. *West Columbus*. Charleston, SC: Arcadia Publishing, 2003.

Lentz, Edward R. *Columbus: A Story of a City*. Charleston, SC: Arcadia Publishing, 2003.

McClure, Stanley. "The Underground Railroad in South Central Ohio." Columbus, Ohio.: Ohio State University, 1932.

McGaw, Judith A. *Early American Technology: Making and Doing Things from the Colonial Era to 1850* : University of North Carolina Press, 1994.

Middleton, Stephen. *The Black Laws: Race and the Legal Process in Early Ohio* Athens, Oh: Ohio University Press, 2005.

Mollenkopf, J. *The Great Black Swamp: Historical Tales of Nineteenth- Century Northwest Ohio*. Toledo, OH: Lake of the Cat Pub, 1999.

Nitchman, Paul E. *Blacks in Ohio, 1880: In the Counties of ...* Decorah, Iowa: P.E. Nitchman, 1985

Peacefull, Leonard. *A Geography of Ohio*. Kent, OH: Kent State University Press, 1996.

Plat Book of Columbus, Ohio and Vicinity. Franklin, TN: Franklin Survey Company.

Porter, L. *Sara's Table: "Keeping House" in Ohio, 1800–1950* Zanesville, OH: New Concord Press, 2001.

Rhodes, James A. *A Short History of Ohio Land Grants, Ohio Auditor of State*. Columbus, OH: F.J. Heer Printing, 1960.

Rothstein, Richard. *The Color of Law,* New York: Liveright Publishing Co., 2017.

Sayer, M. G., ed. *History of Upper Arlington, Sayre, Marjorie, Upper Arlington Historical Society*, 2nd ed. Upper Arlington, OH: Upper Arlington Historical Society, 1988.

Seibert, Wilbur Henry. *Ohio's Underground Trails*. Ohio: A.W. McGraw, 1993.

Seibert, Wilbur Henry. *The Mysteries of Ohio's Underground Railroads* Ohio: A.W. McGraw, 1993.

Siebert, Wilbur Henry. *The Underground Railroad in Ohio* Ohio: A.W. McGraw, 1993.

Smith, John David. *Black Judas: William Hannibal Thomas and the American Negro*. Athens: University of Georgia Press, 2000.

Van Horn-Lane, Janice. *Safe Houses and the Underground Railroad in East Central Ohio*. Charleston, SC: History Press, 2010.

Van Tine, Warren P., and Michael Dale Pierce. *Builders of Ohio: A Biographical History* Columbus: Ohio State University Press, 2003.

Ward, Andrew. *The Slaves' War* Boston, MA: Houghton Mifflin Co., 2008.

White, Ruth Young. *We Too Built Ohio* Columbus, OH: Stoneman Press, 1936.

Williams, G. S. *Gliding to a Better Place: Profiles from Ohio's Territorial Era*. Caldwell, OH: Buckeye Books, 2000.

Williams, James L. *Blazes, Post and Stones: History of Ohio's Original Land Subdivisions*. Akron, OH: University of Akron Press, 2015.

Index

A

Adams, Pres. John – xvii -30- 31
Ambrose, Edwin – 99
AME Church - 99
Anderson, William - 99
Anti-Slavery Baptist
 Church - 92
Armstrong, Louis - 84
Armstrong, Sarah – 38
Arlington Ridge Realty
 Company – 60, 63
Artz – Sallie Thomas – 30
Ashley, Alfred – 99- 100

B

Backus, Elijah – 28-32
Backus Island - 31
Backus, Thomas – 32
Backus Tract – 2
Baldwin, Charles – 76, 79, 82
Baldwin, Rose – 82
Barbershops - 70
Bartgis Republican Gazette – 33
Battle of Brandywine – 43
Battle of Nashville - 62
Battle of Stoney Point – 38
Battle of Trenton – 43

Benevolent Aid Society – 68
Beson, Maria - 60
Bickett's farm – 45
Black Law – 47, 51, 52
Blackberry Patch – 20
Blacksmith – 54-55, 59-60
Blennerhassett, Harmon - 31
Blue Jacket – 6
Board of Education – 68,
 80, 105
Booker, Patsy - 92
Bottoms (Area of Columbus) – 20
Bowers, Charles - 79
Boyd, Edith – 67
Boyd, Timothy Breck - 67
Brandon Heights Addition - 63
Brandon Road – 55, 104
Briggs, Henry - 103
Brigham Young – 58
Brinker, H.W. - 99
Broadhorn – 9
Bryant, C.W. Company - 107
Bryant, Neil – 67
Burgess, Patricia – 97
Burr, Aaron - 31
Butcher, George – 92
Butcher, Mary - 92

C

Camp Chase – 46, 62
Campbell Co, Virginia – 57
Cameroon - 113
Canterbury Place Addition – 100
Capital University – 36
Christian Co, Kentucky - 67
Cincinnati, Ohio – 9
Cincinnati Star - 56
Civil Rights Act of 1965 - 101
Club Litchford - 84
Coffman, Jeanette -30
Colored Cemetery - 104
Colored School – 64-66
Colored Soldiers Relief Society - 68
Columbus Benevolent Society - 48
Columbus City Council – 68, 103
Columbus City Schools - 68
Columbus Museum of Art – 14
Columbus Phone Book - 63
Commodore Perry – 1
Common School Laws - 65
Conestoga Wagon – 12
Convention of Colored Citizens of Ohio - 81
Cook, Nettie – 30
Crosby, Rose – 58
Corduroy Road - 11
Count Basie - 83
Cumberland Road – 13, 50

D

Dam keepers House - 37
Darby Creek - 2
David, Ann Simpson – 29, 42-44
Davis, John- 29, 42-44
Davis Cemetery – 44
Deer Creek - 2
Delashmutt, Anna Marie (Richards) - 36
Delashmutt, Ebenezer – 34
Delashmutt, Elias - 33
Delashmutt, John K. – 33-34
Delashmutt, Van Elias Nelson – 33
Delashmutt, William Trammel – 33-34
Delaware County - 52
Delaware Indians – 7-8
Delaware State Road - 38
Depp, Abraham –62, 88-89
Depp, Aurelius – 60, 62, 89
Depp, Catherine Jane (Litchford) – 89
Depp, China – 88-89
Depp Family – 3, 62-63, 69, 88-89
Depp, Lucy – 62

Depp, Lucinda - 89
Depp, Mary Matilda – 60-61
Dodridge Rd. – 2, 38
Douglas, Nancy – 35
Dublin, Ohio – 3, 42

E

Easley, Matilda Jane - 59
Evans, Frances (Litchford) – 61, 106
Evans, William – 61

F

Fisher, Catherine or Patience (Litchford) - 57-61
Fields, Letha – 92
Fields, Miles – 92
Fields, Shubal - 92
Fields, Rev. Ezekiel – 92, 104, 110
Fisk Caskets – 106-107, 110
Fishel, Ken – 99
Fishinger Road - 2
Flatboat -8-9
Flood, Priscilla - 92
Foley, James - 54
Franklinton – 2, 6, 29, 32-33, 35, 50
Free Soil Party - 53
Friendship Village - 44
Frost, George - 99

G

Galbraith, Elizabeth – 45
Gallipolis, Ohio - 9
Gardener, William - 92
Gilford Road - 63
Goode Family - 52
(Gen.) Grant, Ulysses -43
Grandview - 1
Graves, Clinton – 74, 77
Green Flakes – 57-58
Green, Harry L. - 105
Greenlawn Cemetery – 39, 59-60, 104, 105
Griswold, Ezra - 38
Griswold, Rose - 38

H

Hannah Neil Mission and Home for the Friendless – 48
Hayes, Pres. Rutherford B. - 68
Hickman, William E. - 66
Hilton, Chief (Police officer) – 74-78
History of Upper Arlington - 101
Hutchinson, Amaziah – 28-30
Hutchinson, Daniel – 28
Hutchinson, Elizabeth Mack - 28
Hutchinson, (Capt.) Eleazer – 28
Hutchinson, Kate - 30
Hutchinson, Laura Thomas – 30

I

Imhoff, Paul - 112
Industrial Revolution – 25-26
Iron Load Big Cottonwood
    Mine - 58

J

Jacob Slyh Road - 2
James, Etta – 83
Johnson, Charles F. – 95-96
Jones, Edith Alicia – 66
Jones, Clarence Alexander – 67
Jones, Wilbur - 109

K

Kelly, Alfred – 6-7
Kenny Road – 55
King, B.B. – 84
Kittles, Dr. Rick - 113

L

Lakin, Daniel - 38
Lakin, David – 2
Lakin, Emmaline Owen – 38
Lakin, George - 80
Lakin, S.W. - 58
LeBlanc, Nicholas –22
Legg, Amason – 41-42
Legg, Effie – 41-42
Legg Elijah – 39-40
Legg, James – 54
Legg, John - 54
Legg – Lewis – 41-42
Legg, Mildred – 41-42
Legg, Orrell – 41-42
Legg, Susannah –39
Legg, Thomas – 40-42
Legg Walcott Cemetery - 40
LeVeque Tower – 14
Lincoln, Abraham – 53, 69
Little Miami River – 7
Litchford, Abraham –53, 60
Litchford, Ardena – 55-57, 61,
Litchford, Catherine or Patience
    (Fisher) – 57- 61
Litchford - Catherine Jane – 57,
    89
Litchford Cemetery – 57, 61,
    104-105, 107, 109, 110
Litchford, Charlotte (Lottie)
    Stewart –56, 64
Litchford, Fannie – 59, 63
Litchford, Fredrick A. – 49,
    57- 60
Litchford, Frances Evans –55,
    106-107
Litchford, Elias –57-59
Litchford, Emma - 60
Litchford, Eugene -109
Litchford, Grant – 109

Litchford, Irdenia - 60
Litchford, James – 109
Litchford Hotel – 76, 83-87
Litchford Cocktail Lounge – 84-85
Litchford, Lydia – 58, 109
Litchford, Mabella – 57, 105
Litchford, Maria – 63, 107
Litchford, Mariah – 74, 105
Litchford, Matilda, Jane (Easley) – 59, 83
Litchford, Miles – 49, 52, 57- 58, 72, 81
Litchford Sr. Pleasant – xv, xvi, 2, 3, 47, 49-67, 69, 87, 104-109, 113
Litchford, Pleasant Blake – 57, 60, 71, 73, 75,
Litchford, Sarah – 57, 59, 62
Litchford, Susan -135
Litchford Township Road – 2, 68-79, 94
Litchford (Litchferd), William - 83-85, 87
Little Miami River – 4
Log cabin - 16
Log house – 16-17
Loving School – 62
Loving, Sterling - 62
Lucy Depp Settlement – 61, 62-63, 88-89

M
Mable Cliff Mill – 1, 32
Mack, Elizabeth - 29
Manumisson Papers - 50
Matere's Mill – 32
Madison, Indiana - 55-56, 61
Marietta, Ohio – 9, 31
Martin, Billy - 107
McCoy's Mill – 32
McCoy, James – 35, 40
McCoy, Hugh - 40
McCoy, Robert – 35-36
McElvin, A. - 2
Miller, Henry – 2,7
Miller, James – 96, 103
Miller farm - 52
Milton, New York - 28
Mississippi River – 8-9
Monroe, Pres. James, - 88
Muskingham River - 4

N
National Road- 5-8, 10-17, 46, 50, 67, 69, 87, 89
National Pike – 11-12
Negro Motorist Green Book – 101-102
Neil, Hannah – 47-48
Neil, Robert - 54
Neil, William – 46-48, 54

New Orleans - 8
Northam Park – 55
North Graveyard - 103
North Star Road – 101
Northwest Blvd.- 101
Northwest Arlington Homeowners Association – xv, 96-100

O
Oberlin College – 62, 89
Ohio –Erie Canal – 6
Ohio Gazette - 31
Ohio House of Representative - 6
Ohio River – 5-9, 30, 46, 50
Ohio Real Estate Commission – 99
Ohio School for the Blind - 68
Ohio Statehouse – 54
Ohio State University – 65, 67
Olentangy Post Office – 3
Olentangy River - 5
Otterbein College - 87

P
Pace, John H. - 99
Palace Theater – 14
Parkersburg, W. Va. - 30
Patterson, John - 83
Perrin, Joseph – 29
Perry Township – 39
Perry Township Board of Education – 52, 64
Phelps, Ella – 75-83
Pheneger, Rudolph –34, 45
Planned Communities Inc. - 44
Poindexter, James – 66, 69, 80-81, 92
Poindexter, Richard – 67
Poindexter Village - 69
Pott, Chris - 112
Powhatan Co, Virginia – 60
Primitive Baptist Church - 34
Prince William County, Virginia – 39
Prophet -6

Q

R
Randall, Phoebe - 92
Range Nineteen – 1
Revolutionary War – 40, 96
Richards, Cleanthis – 33
Richards, Ester (Richards) - 33
Richards, Hiram – 2, 36-37
Richards, Julius - 36
Richards, Ziphorah – 35
Ridgeview Road – 2, 63, 64, 68, 78, 79, 94, 104

Reitalbach, Albin C. - 97
Rope bed - 18

S
Salt Lake City - 58
Second Baptist Church – 52-53, 64-66, 101, 103-104, 110
Sellsville, Ohio – 52
Schuylkill River – 42
Schweikart, John - 112
Scioto River –4-8, 40, 63, 96
Scots-Irish - 2
Shawnee Indians - 6
Shelley v. Kraemer - 100
Simmons, Christine, - 67
Simmons, Loren Few – 67
Simmons, Dr. John – 67
Slyh, Daniel Mathias – 38
Slyh, Emmaline Harriett - 38
Slyh, Henry T - 38
Slyh, Jacob Edward– 2, 38
Slyh, John William – 38
Slyh, Mary - 37
Slyh, Mary Elizabeth - 38
Slyh, Mathias - 37
Slyh, Mary Elizabeth – 38
Slyh, Rebecca Ruth - 38
Slyh, Serena Ann – 38
Smith, Cleanthis - 33
Smith, (Richards), Lois – 33
State Convention of Colored Citizens of Ohio -65
State Employees Retirement System - 8
Stewart, Charlotte (Lottie) – 56
Stillman, Wyllys -31
Sullivan, David – 92,103
Sullivan, Joseph – 88
Sullivan, Lucas – 88
Sullivan, Susan - 92
Sundown town – xvi, 52, 101
Swain Family – 52
Swain, Edon – 107-108

T
Tecumseh -6
Thomas, Laura Hutchinson - 30
Thomas, William Hannibal – 86-87
Thompson, Ben – 95, 103
Thompson, King – 95, 98-99, 103
Tikar tribe - 113
Toledo and Columbus Railroad - 3
Tremont Elementary School – 55
Tremont Road – 39
Truitt, Karen – 112

U

Underground Railroad – 3, 61-65, 69
Union Army – 59
Union Cemetery – 34, 36, 38, 57, 92, 105, 107, 111
Union Depot - 37
U.S. Military Lands – 31-32, 39, 40, 45, 48, 96
Upper Arlington Bd of Education – 104-105, 111
Upper Arlington Public Library - 55
Upper Arlington Senior Center – 52, 56, 64

V

Valley Forge - 43
Vandalia, Illinois – 11
Virginia Military Tract – 31, 32, 96

W

Walcott, Absalom - 38
Walcott, Amelia -38
Walcott, Harrison – 38
Walcott, John - 38
Walcott, Louisa – 38
Walcott, Robert – 38-40
Walcott, Thomas – 51
Walhonding Trail – 5-6
Walcott, William – 39-40
Walker, Catherine Litchford – 72- 83
Walker, J. R. - 72
Warrior's Path – 8
(Gen.) Washington, George – 43
Washington, Pastor Howard – 93-94
Washington, Minister Floria - 94
Watson, Susan – 92
Wellington School - 39
Western Reserve Historical Society -7
Wetherbee, Hannah – 41
Whyte, Dr. Samuel – 89
Wilberforce College – 68
Wilson, Nancy – 84, 85
Woodson, Sarah - 92
Worthington, Ohio – 1, 28

X

Y

Yale College - 40
Yeager, William - 99

Z

Zinn, Clyde - 42
Zinn, Helen Legg - 42
Zinn, Harvey - 42
Zollinger Road – 55

Disclaimer for historical materials

This book contains historical materials that may contain offensive language or negative stereotypes reflecting the culture or language of a period or place. This book is presenting these items as part of the historical record.

About the Authors

Diane Kelly Runyon is a member of the Association of Professional Genealogists, and the Ulster Foundation in Northern Ireland. Diane was a teacher for thirty years and was awarded Ohio History's Teacher of the Year in 2012. History is her passion, and she is a scholar of Irish genealogy. She continues her postgraduate studies in early American life at Yale University. As a lifelong historian, she studies the lives of those who have gone before us. She is the owner of Lineage Links LLC, a genealogical and historical research firm. Diane lives in Noblesville, Indiana.

Kim Shoemaker Starr is a gravestone restoration specialist. Kim has restored numerous cemeteries throughout the United States. Recently she worked on the headstones at Davis Cemetery in Upper Arlington. Her accomplishments in volunteerism have been recognized statewide and nationally. In 2016, Kim was bestowed the Historic Preservation Recognition Award. She is a member of the Colonial Dames. Kim is the owner of Shine on with Love, gravesite restoration and care company. Kim was born, raised, and now resides in Upper Arlington, Ohio.

Diane and Kim are both members of the Daughters of the American Revolution

Emmy Award Winning Production

The Pleasant Litchford Story won an Emmy Award for best Magazine Feature Segment – WOSU. 2019 Charlene Brown, Mary Rathke, Ryan Hitchcock, Ben Bays and Gary Orr.

Program can be seen on YouTube.